St. Thérèse
Doctor of the Little Way

Imprimatur: ✠ Most Rev. Sean Patrick O'Malley, O.F.M. Cap.
Bishop of Fall River, Massachusetts, USA
Dec. 12, 1997 – Our Lady of Guadalupe

The nihil obstat and imprimatur are official declarations that a book or pamphlet is free from doctrinal or moral error. No implication is contained therein that those who granted the nihil obstat or imprimatur agree with the contents or statements expressed.

OUR COVER: St. Thérèse, holding pictures of the Child Jesus and the Holy Face which summarizes her special devotion and spirituality. They are also included in her religious name. The title of the book, St. Thérèse, Doctor of the Little Way, seems to be appropriate since that is what the book is all about — the spirituality of the little way of spiritual childhood. The background writing is a facsimile of a page from her Story of a Soul. This picture of St. Thérèse was taken June 7, 1897, when she was already weak and enduring much suffering.

Park Press, Inc., P.O. Box 475, 355 6th Ave. N., Waite Park, MN 56387

*"I have not given the good God any-
thing but love, and it is with love he
will repay. After my death, I will let
fall a shower of roses. I will spend my
heaven in doing good upon earth.*

*My 'little way' is the way of spiri-
tual childhood, the way of trust and
absolute self-surrender."*

St. Thérèse:
Doctor of the Little Way

Franciscan Friars of the Immaculate
Our Lady's Chapel, New Bedford, MA, USA

Acknowledgements

There are always many people involved behind the scenes in putting together a book such as *St. Thérèse, Doctor of the Little Way*. First and foremost in this hidden involvement are friars of my community who have shown great interest in the latest book. Since we began *St. Thérèse, Doctor of the Little Way*, it seemed I saw more copies of *Story of a Soul* in the Friar's places in chapel. The editor relied more than ever before on the community for help. From the superior, Fr. Peter Fehlner, who not only gave his encouragement and devoted much of his precious time to check out each chapter for accuracy and orthodoxy, to our printery Friars, who supplied the necessary expertise in scanning, setting and composing pages of the book.

Special thanks to Fra Fidelis who, besides composing the pages, pulled the editor out of many a mishap on the computer. Father Martin, busy as he is with many projects, designed the attractive front and back covers of the book. Fra Maximilian and Fr. Thomas Huff, in line with their commitment to our Marian vow of total consecration to Our Lady, contributed important Marian chapters to the book.

The Carmelites were very well represented with contributions by the first, second and third Order members. Two local Secular Carmelites, Louise Roberge, who translated Bishop Gaucher's Preface from French into English, and Susan Muldoon who wrote the article *St. Thérèse: Light in the Culture of Death* were last minute contacts who also made great sacrifices to help the editor. Indeed, Our Lady's projects always entail much sacrifice.

Scarcely four months before our deadline in November we were put in contact with a Carmelite priest in San Antonio, Texas, Fr. Louis Scagnelli, OCD, through an old friend of ours of over thirty years, Fr. Herbert Schmidt, who also supplied much initial help with his suggestions. Fr. Louis gave us the names of Mary Ann Budnik and the Kochiss brothers. They were contacted at the last moment. Mary Ann contributed the chapter on the parents of St. Thérèse and did a fine job meeting a very a short deadline.

The Kochiss twins, Joseph and John, drove over two hundred miles each way, three times within a month to New Bedford bringing with them much valuable research material that we drew from, especially for illustrations. The proofreading this time was done by a very competent proofreader, Kit O'Brien, who proofreads for other publications.

Last and certainly not least our gratitude to the two bishops, Bishop Sean O'Malley, O.F.M. Cap. who again gave his imprimatur to the book and Bishop Guy Gaucher, O.C.D., who wrote the Preface. Bishop Gaucher, Auxiliary Bishop of the diocese where Lisieux is located, busy as he was with both the centenary celebration and Thérèse being declared a Doctor of the Church took time to send us a faxed Preface. Coming as it did from the foremost authority on Thérèsian research and spirituality, we were especially pleased by this endorsement of *St. Thérèse, Doctor of the Little Way*.

Contents

Buildings associated with St. Thérèse, top to bottom: Basilica of St. Thérèse in Lisieux, convent of Carmelites where she lived and died, Les Buissonets where she grew up, Saint-Pierre, Cathedral in Lisieux, Notre Dame Church where she was baptized.

Saints and Marian Shrines, No 2
Introduction

The *St. Thérèse: Doctor of the Little Way* book is the second in a series of books, *Saints and Marian Shrines* (the first *A Handbook On Guadalupe*). It is providentially well timed. This year, besides being the centenary year of her death, is the one in which she has been honored by being declared the 33rd Saint named a Doctor of the Universal Church. You may be sure that we didn't plan this book to coincide with these two great Church events, but are convinced that they (both Our Lady and St. Thérèse) had much to do with it.

Personally, I have felt for many years that St. Thérèse would be thus recognized some day for her great contribution to spirituality and theology in modern times. I was far from being alone in anticipating her being declared a Doctor of the Church. The National Conference of Catholic Bishops at their 11th Episcopal Conference in November of 1993 requested of the Holy Father that he confer on her the title Doctor of the Church. Bishop Patrick Ahern, auxiliary bishop New York, who was the leader in this effort, addressed his fellow Bishops on that occasion, pointing out that St. Thérèse is "one of our own.... Thérèse walked the same road we travel," and added, "This is the doctor of the Church we need today....one who speaks today's language and addresses the age . . .through which we are living."

Since then each American Cardinal while making his official visit to the Holy Father has reiterated this request. Nor were the American Bishops alone; over fifty National Conferences of Bishops worldwide made this request. Cardinal O'Connor of New York presented a formal petition to the Holy Father together with a position paper justifying Thérèse's Doctorate. Besides the hierarchy, huge numbers of lay people all over the world have petitioned the Pope to bestow this honor on the Saint whom Pope St. Pius X called, "the greatest saint of modern times." Pope John Paul II, as a Carmelite tertiary and great admirer of St. Thérèse and Carmelite Spirituality, was more than pleased to bestow this honor on the nineteenth century religious (see pages 66-72).

We Franciscan Friars of the Immaculate, publishers of the book, followers of St. Francis of Assisi and St. Maximilian Kolbe, are indeed privileged to be able to publish a book in English on St. Thérèse so soon after her being named a Doctor of the Church. Despite differences between the rule and life of the Cammelites and Franciscans, there is a close kinship between the Franciscan Order and the Carmelites. In fact it was a Franciscan Friar, St. Peter of Alcantara, who encouraged and directed St. Theresa of Avila in her successful reform efforts in the sixteenth century.

The important and universal message of St. Thérèse for our day is that personal holiness is for everyone, clerical as well as religious, lay apostles and priests, missionaries and contemplative nuns. In a sense, she anticipated Vatican Council II's reminder that holiness is for everyone. One of the four marks of the true Church established by Christ is holiness—holiness in its Founder, in its purpose and in its members. The Catholic Church has radiated holiness in its members in every century, among the young and old, peasants and kings, covering every imaginable vocation and all nationalities. Mother Theresa of Calcutta is a striking example in our day. And surely we need such examples before us to give us hope in a hopeless age, which can benefit so immensely from the inspiration of their heroic and selfless love of God and fellow man.

It is said that where evil abounds, good abounds that much more. St. Thérèse is a case in point. The French have produced some pretty influential and well-known philosophers, writers, etc. in the last hundred years who have attacked the Church and caused considerable confusion in our times. Some did so openly in attacking the Church and its beliefs, others in a much more insidious way, by remaining within the Church and biding their time to openly dissent from Church teachings and were thus more destructive. But this unknown Carmelite nun who died at 24, at the very moment most people are beginning their careers, was raised up by God at a time when intellectualism and pride were running rampant. St. Thérèse of the Infant Jesus and the Holy Face directs us back to the Gospel and to the solution of our problems, given in Scripture, "Unless you become as little children you shall not enter the kingdom of heaven" (Mt. 18:3).

As Bishop Sheen used to quote from Scripture, "the Devil has his hour" but the final word is with God. The Church is experiencing a terrible crisis of faith in our times. Dissent is rampant, but at the same time God is raising up great Saints. St. Thérèse bears out the fact that the Catholic Church is still busy producing, not only canonized Saints but, many holy people, unrecognized but following in Thérèse's footsteps. They are obedient like the humble "handmaid of the Lord" (Lk. 1:48) and adhere to the voice of Christ as expressed by Holy Mother the Church and our spiritual Mother, Mary, who at Cana told the servants and through them, all of us, "Do whatever He tells you" (Jn. 2: 5).

In conclusion: our ardent hope is that this modest work will stimulate the reader to pick up and read A Story of a Soul, and be inspired to seek that which is the whole purpose of life—personal holiness through the practice of the Little Way of Spiritual Childhood. We believe that if this in fact happens, we will have accomplished all that we wish for, to produce something more than just another work among the many books already available on St. Thérèse. "St. Thérèse, Doctor of the Little Way, pray for us!"

Bro. Francis Mary, F.I., Editor

Preface

As we enter this Centenary year studying the life of St. Thérèse of the Child Jesus and the Holy Face, we experience an event whose consequences are yet too difficult to evaluate, or perhaps too profound to fathom: the proclamation of her being raised to a Doctor of the Church by Pope John Paul II on Mission Sunday, October 19. One hundred years after St. Thérèse's passion and death in the infirmary of a small, obscure Carmel, the Pope points out that the prestigious title of Doctor conferred upon her is "in response to countless requests, and careful study."

But what is a Doctor of the Church? Three conditions are necessary to become a Doctor of the Church:

1) One must be a canonized saint. Sister Thérèse was canonized on May 17, 1925 by Pope Pius XI.

2) The candidate must give to the Church a theological, spiritual teaching of "eminent doctrine" — clearly orthodox — and beneficial to the universal Church. This is what must be examined and proven to the experts, theologians of the Sacred Congregation of the Faith and the Cause of the Saints, and finally to the Cardinals of both of these Congregations. A voluminous dossier of 978 pages — called a "Positio" — was humbly and prayerfully compiled by twelve historians and theologians. After very careful study and irrefutable evidence the "Positio" was sent to the office of Pope John Paul II.

3) The Holy Father decided to declare this young Carmelite, who died at the age of 24, a Doctor of the Church, thus fulfilling the third condition. Thérèse, therefore, becomes the 33rd Doctor of the Church and the third woman, joining the company of St. Teresa of Avila of Spain, and St. Catherine of Siena of Italy—both declared Doctors by Pope Paul VI in 1970. In Paris at the International World Youth Day, Pope John Paul II read briefly from this huge dossier, stating the reasons for his decision:

"Thérèse's teaching, a veritable science of love, is the luminous expression of her understanding of the mystery of Christ, and her personal response to that grace. She inspires men and women of today and those of tomorrow to better perceive God's gifts and spread the Good News of His infinite Love. . . ."

A Carmelite, apostle, teacher of spiritual wisdom to many consecrated souls and to the laity, patroness of the missions — Saint Thérèse occupies a special place in the Church. Her eminent doctrine merits to be recognized among the most fruitful."

In 1925, Pope Pius XI had already declared that Saint Thérèse of Lisieux was "a word from God meant for the whole world." It is a fact that this young saint has effected a profound influence on the entire world for the past hundred years; a spiritual impact on countless people who discovered Jesus and the Gospel through her; a theological effect that influenced great theologians of this century, from Cardinal Yves Congar to Fr. Urs von Balthasar, including Cardinals Journet, Garrone, Danielou, spiritual writers such as Frs. Combes and Marie-Eugene of the Child Jesus, also including philosophers like Bergson, Mounier, Maritain, Daujat, Guitton; and writers such as Claudel, Bernanos, Mauriac, Julien Green, Daniel Rops, Marie-Noel, and above all the saints and the blessed like Elizabeth of the Trinity, Fr. Maximilian Kolbe, Fr. Brottier, Edith Stein and many others.

What astounds me about Thérèse, who never wrote a single theological treatise, is that the Holy Spirit inspired her writings (manuscripts, letters, poems, play), set down under obedience, mirroring her life, in utter transparency: "I never sought anything but the Truth." She spoke of the Trinity, the Father, Jesus, and the Holy Spirit in the simplest terms, which were translated into sixty languages and thus available to all; she focused everything on the word of God and Scripture; she understood that before all else, the Church is a Communion of Love: "In the Heart of the Church, my mother, I shall be love."

She stated with conviction that Mary of Nazareth was no mere marginal person to whom we simply show devotion, but placed Our Lady at the heart of the mystery of Christ; and that the Communion of Saints unites heaven and earth. She lived the dark night of faith, "seated at the table of sinners" so that her unbelieving or doubting brothers would come to accept the light of Faith and Hope. She was consumed with concern for the mission of the Church.

We can safely say that she was one of the heralds who paved the way for the Second Vatican Council. In the Catechism of the Catholic Church, she is quoted six times in very strategic places. In the history of humanity and the Church nothing has ever been accomplished without the contribution of both men and women. In the astounding revelation of Divine Mercy, no one ever went to greater lengths to bring to life the truths of the Incarnation than the holy women we find with Mary on the road to Calvary and at the foot of the cross, refuting the Gnostic ramblings. It is therefore a great joy for the Church and for Thérèse's countless friends worldwide, to have this young woman declared a Doctor of the Church, at the dawn of the third millennium, in preparation for the Jubilee Year 2000.

The Gospels give a profound sense of "the mystery of God revealed to the little ones and to the poor, hidden from the wise and clever of the world." With startling audacity Sister Thérèse of the Child Jesus and the Holy Face dared to paraphrase the Gospel of Matthew 5:3 in these words:

"Ah! so astounding is it to see a child of fourteen years understand the secrets of perfection, secrets that men with all their science cannot fathom since to possess them one must be poor in spirit!"

St. Thérèse of Lisieux, who had written: "Ah! despite my littleness, I desire to enlighten souls like the Prophets and Doctors; I have the vocation to be an apostle..." Here she is a teacher of all nations, revealing to them the secrets of God's Merciful Love. The following text of the Old Testament encompasses all that relates perfectly to her, "I will make the instruction shine like the dawn and diffuse its light far beyond. I will spread the teaching like a prophecy and bequeath it to future generations" (Sir. 24:32-34). No vain intellectual or abstract teachings, the Little Way, but passionate revelations of the mysteries of life which give meaning to our existence, and open the path to eternal life.

We also hope that those people who are not very familiar with Thérèse of Lisieux, having always thought of her as "the Little Saint of the Roses," harmless and rather dull, will reconsider their superficial impressions and discover the depth of her writings and the power of her living testimony. With the arrival of new generations, we are at the dawn of a new stage in Thérèsian research. The simplicity of "Little Thérèse" will not be overshadowed by this illustrious title. Though now a Doctor of the Church, she remains in utmost simplicity, according to her desire, Patroness of the Missions, Patroness of the Mission of France, Patroness of Novitiates, Patroness of Catholic Action and Secondary Patroness of France.

In her brief life, she had no other motive but "to love the Trinity and make It loved." Her life was totally centered on Jesus "her only Love who led her to the Father through the gentleness and power of the Holy Spirit." She wrote: "I understand and I know from experience 'that the kingdom of God dwells within us.' Jesus has neither need of books nor doctors to instruct souls. He, the Doctor of doctors, instructs without the sound of words... Never have I heard him speak but I sense that He is within me; at each moment, He guides and inspires me in what I should say and do."

As early as 1932, one of Thérèse's most ardent admirers, the saintly Carmelite Father Marie Eugene of the Child Jesus declared: "She, a little child, will teach the souls who will make up the army of the last days which will give themselves over entirely to God's mercy. We are at the start of her mission. The great works are still to come, and they will show her at last for what she really is, a great among all the saints!" She has promised to work for us, "to the end of time." This is clear enough. God always finishes what He begins.

Guy Gaucher, Auxiliary Bishop of Bayeux and Lisieux

A painting by Sister Marie of the Holy Spirit, a Carmelite of Lisieux, of the canonization of St. Thérèse at St. Peter's Basilica in Rome, May 17, 1925.

The Little Way

By Msgr. Vernon Johnson

In ordinary human life, what is the supreme relationship between a little child and its mother? It is love. It is the mother's love that has brought the little child into being, and by its mother's love it is supported every moment. Above all, the thing which the mother wants supremely from her little child is its love. If she possesses all else but does not possess that, her heart is left aching. Now, from the point of view of the little one, what does the little child want? It wants love. Without its mother's love it is not merely restless, it is completely lost. Again, in its helplessness the only gift that the little child can give to its mother is its love. Between a mother and her child all is love, and if this should not exist, then all society cries out in horror that things are wrong.

Now in the supernatural life this is precisely, theologically true. God is our heavenly Father. He has created us because He loves us. By His love we are supported every moment. The one thing which this heavenly Father wants from us, His children, is our love. Without it, His heart is left aching. We, on our side, we, His little children, we want supremely the love of our heavenly Father. Without it we are restless and dissatisfied. Why is the world so unhappy? Because it is trying to satisfy itself with something less than the love of God.

In the eyes of St. Thérèse this was everything: "My Little Way is all love." Sometimes it is the love of her heavenly Father which absorbs her; her continual cry was "God thirsts for our love." At other times it is the love of her own heart; her love goes out in response to her Father's love. "Let us love," she writes, "for love alone our hearts are made." Sometimes it is the two together which captivate her soul. "Oh, my God, I know it. Love is repaid by love alone. Therefore I have sought, I have found how to ease my heart by giving You love for love." We depend upon Him for our existence but, far more important still, we owe entirely to Him the capacity which we possess to love Him in the only way which can satisfy His heart. "Let us love God because God first has loved us" (1 Jn 4:19). That is the order. The little, that is to say, childlike soul, who treads the Little Way, looking at its heavenly Father, puts aside all His other attributes, His omniscience, His omnipotence, and sees just one overwhelming thing, His love.

This, then, is the first foundation of the Little Way of Spiritual Childhood. To those who walk in this Little Way all is love between the heavenly Father and His child; and it is precisely the little, childlike soul that, putting aside all other truths that might complicate its vision, goes straight to the heart of things and sees just the overwhelming truth of the Father's love. To the little soul the whole burden of Scripture is the coming down of the Father's love to dwell in the soul of His little child, and so lift it up to Him; and the whole of the Catholic Church, its hierarchy and its sacraments, exist for one purpose and one end, namely, the planting of that seed of divine love in each individual soul. And therefore it is the Blessed Sacrament which is, above all, the center and the inspiration of the Little Way, because in it this truth is focused to a point with such complete simplicity. And it is the little soul which, with its complete simplicity of outlook, sees this most directly; just as in the case of a little child, the only thing it sees in its parent is love.

And what is littleness in a soul? It is humility. Humility is the virtue which enables us to see how utterly dependent we are upon the heavenly Father. And so St. Thérèse loved humility above all else. It was the essential foundation of her Little Way. That is why the Little Way is so sure, so safe. Pride and humility in deadly conflict, that is the whole process of redemption. To be emptied of self so as to be filled with the divine love needs a new birth, a conversion. "Unless you be converted and become as little children you cannot enter the kingdom of Heaven" (Mt: 18: 3). As pride is the root of all sin, making us think we can live independently of God and thereby separating us from Him, teaching us, in fact, to let go the heavenly Father's hand, so humility is the foundation of all holiness, teaching us our essential dependence upon God, placing our hand once again firmly in that of the heavenly Father.

And so St. Thérèse learned to be glad at the knowledge of her failings just because that taught her littleness, which was so precious in her eyes because it was so precious to our Lord. "That which pleases Jesus in my little soul is to see me love my littleness," the littleness which enabled her to keep firm hold of her Father's hand. This humility is no weak or negative thing. It is the most powerful thing in the world, for it is the key which unlocks the soul to grace. By ourselves we can do nothing to increase in us the supernatural love for which we were made, but by grace we help by removing that which is in the way of the divine love, namely, self-love. With every act of humility, every time we accept a humiliation lovingly, more of self is removed, and therefore there is more room for the divine love to dwell in the soul.

From humility springs the next foundation of the Little Way of Spiritual Childhood. In the natural sphere, what is it that springs from the dependence of the little child? Out of its utter dependence springs an unquestioning confidence. The mysteries of our Holy Faith, which are the proofs to the little, humble soul of the heavenly Father's love, are also to the humble soul the grounds of its confidence. Bethlehem, Calvary, the Resurrection, the indwelling of the Holy Trinity in the soul, the Blessed Sacrament, all spell one word, confidence. "He that spared not even his own Son, but delivered Him up for us all, how has He not also, with Him, given us all things?" (Rom. 8:32). It was this that gave St. Thérèse her invincible confidence. "My Way is all love and confidence in God. I cannot understand those souls who are afraid of so tender a friend. . . .What offends Jesus, what wounds Him to the heart, is our want of confidence. . . .We cannot have too much confidence in the good God, so mighty, so merciful."

To St. Thérèse the heavenly Father's love is supremely a merciful love. Just because she was so conscious of her littleness and weakness she saw, with a clearness impossible to a soul less conscious of its weakness, that the supreme quality of the heavenly Father's love was its mercy. Her soul's delight was to meditate on the merciful love of God Incarnate stooping down to earth and reaching out to that which is weakest, most soiled, most miserable. That, to her, was the supreme motive of the merciful love of God, namely, pity for that which is weak. She knew her weakness would cry to the heavenly Father's mercy as nothing else could do. From this sprang her invincible confidence. She says: "Indeed, I hope as much from the justice of God as from His mercy. It is because He is just that He is compassionate and merciful, long-suffering, plenteous in mercy. For He knows our frame, He remembers that we are but dust. 'As the father has compassion on His children, so has the Lord compassion on us.' What joy to think that our Lord is just, that He takes into account all our weaknesses and He knows perfectly all the frailty of our nature. How, then, can I be afraid?

"I am certain that, even if I had on my conscience every imaginable sin, I should lose nothing of my confidence, but would throw myself, heartbroken with sorrow, into the arms of my Savior. I remember His love for the Prodigal Son; I have heard His words to Mary Magdalene, to the woman taken in adultery, and to the woman of Samaria. No, there is no one who could frighten me, for I know too well what to believe concerning His mercy and His love."

But if, on the one hand, the Little Way gives confidence to great sinners, it also gives confidence to those who are tortured by scruples because of their little failings. In the natural sphere "little children do not fall very far, and, if they do fall, they do not hurt themselves very much, and the mother's arms are round them almost before they fall." St. Thérèse tells us it is the same in the spiritual sphere. In fact these little failings and miseries can be turned into a blessing, for they teach the little soul its weakness and so throw it back once more into its Father's arms. "What does it matter to me to fall each moment? By that I feel my weakness and therein I find great profit. My God, you see what I can do if You do not carry me in your arms."

Every Christian knows the philosophy of living just for today; how, if we live for today, it lessens the power of our temptations, because we are tempted only for today; how it takes away the power of pain if we have to suffer only for today. But St. Thérèse, with her Little Way, throws completely new light on it. For she says that all this is secondary, that the real thing is to think of today as the only day we have in which to love God. What quality then will we put into our love! If we love Him today as though we had no other day in which to love Him, then of course, automatically, all our pain becomes easier to bear, all our temptations lose their strength. But it is the love which is the key to it all. "I notice," she says, "that our Lord does not give me provisions, but nourishes me from moment to moment with food that is ever new. I do not know how it happens, but I just believe that it is Jesus, hidden in the depth of my soul, inspiring me and giving me the power, moment by moment, to do what He wishes."

A little child relates everything to its mother in little acts of love. And, all the time, it can only do it because its mother is there, watching it, supporting it with her care and ready to receive its offering. Without her its love would have no object; all would be chaos and confusion. In the Little Way of Spiritual Childhood it is precisely the same. The little soul can only cooperate with the Father's love, can only express its own love by little things, by relating everything to the heavenly Father as an expression of its love. Thus, she took every little incident, every joy, every disappointment and misunderstanding, everything that came her way, some little word or action, something easy, something difficult, she grasped each, as a little child plucks a flower, and laid it at our Lord's feet as an expression of her love for Him. "I work for His pleasure alone."

This entirely puts an end to the temptation to divide our life into spiritual and secular, the temptation to think of God only when we are upon our knees and to forget Him in our work. Everything is an instrument to express our love, every humiliation taken patiently, every difficulty faced calmly, every sorrow borne courageously, every disappointment met bravely, every weary detail taken cheerily, every little duty in the home or business done to the best of our ability, all of these are offerings, little flowers by which to express our love of our heavenly Father. The little soul makes these acts of love just as much in the gray days as in the days when all is bright and sunny. "In times of dryness when I am incapable of praying and practicing virtue, I seek little opportunities, mere trifles, to give pleasure to Jesus: for instance, a smile, a pleasant word when inclined to show weariness. If I have no opportunities I at least tell Him again and again that I love Him."

Next to our love for our heavenly Father comes our love for our neighbor, those men and women with whom we live our daily life. The source of St. Thérèse's love to those around her was the supernatural love which the heavenly Father placed in the soul of His child. "Oh, my Jesus, you never ask what is impossible. You know I can never love my sisters as you have loved them unless within me you love them, dear Lord . . . . Yes, I know when I show charity to others it is simply Jesus acting in me, and the more closely I am united to Him the more dearly I love my sisters." So only can the little soul fulfill our Blessed Lord's commandment: "Little children, love one another, as 1 have loved you" (Jn 13:34). By this the little soul is saved from all those unworthy motives which destroy the peace of so many — jealousies, envies, criticisms, scandals.

The little soul sees others only in their relationship to their heavenly Father. Apart from this, it is unmoved by their actions, their motives, their temperaments, whether they be attractive or otherwise. The little child does not judge. "Is there anything more sweet," says St. Thérèse, "than the inward joy of thinking well of our neighbor?" This sounds too high an ideal for human nature. It is indeed only those souls who are little enough to see only the Father's love that can attain to it.

So she trod her Little Way with childlike confidence right to the end.

This chapter and the related chapter "Abandonment in Suffering," (page 46) are excerpted from the excellent little booklet, "Spiritual Childhood," by Msgr. Johnson (see bibliography page 162).

6

MYSTICAL SIMPLICITY

By CANON PAUL TRAVERT
The Late Chaplain of the Carmel of Lisieux

" Behold the greatest saint of modern times ! " -St. Pius X

We might debate at length upon the meaning of this pronounce-
ment, were it not that on two occasions the saintly Pope defined the reasons for his admiration of the Saint of Lisieux. One day a priest, seeking
to convince the Holy Father that there was nothing extraordinary in the
life of this saint, received the following reply: *"Ah! What is most extraordinary of all in her life is precisely her extreme simplicity. Consult your
theology!"*

This is the first point. In the view of Pope St. Pius X, St. Thérèse
of the Child Jesus is a great saint for the very reason that her spirituality

**Let the little children come to me: for the kingdom of heaven is for such (Mt
19: 14). Unless you become as little children, you shall not enter the kingdom of heaven (Mt 18: 3).**

is extremely simple, and, adds the Supreme Pontiff, such is the teaching of the Church: "Consult your theology." There is a need in our day to bring this theological lesson to light once more.

The second point which impressed this same Pope concerning St. Thérèse' sanctity is revealed in the following episode. Msgr. de Teil, vice-postulator of the cause of the Saint, had shown the Holy Father a letter written by the young Carmelite to her cousin Marie Guerin, who was allowing scruples to keep her away from Holy Communion. Here St. Thérèse warns all the scrupulous against the wiles of Satan "who seeks to deprive Jesus of a loved tabernacle, well knowing that he will then have won the victory over this poor heart, empty without its Lord." The reaction of Pope Pius X to this letter is described in the following passage: "'Opportunissimo! Opportunissimo!' he exclaimed on reading the opening lines; then, addressing Msgr. de Teil, 'This is a great joy to me, we must use all speed in dealing with this process.'"

The supernatural simplicity of St. Thérèse of the Child Jesus and her enlightened love for the Holy Eucharist, wherein she discerns the means par excellence of withstanding the devil and securing the strength of Our Blessed Lord Himself are then, in the eyes of St. Pius X, the two things which prompt him to declare her "the greatest saint of modern times." The teaching of St. Thérèse provides a corrective for many errors, if not of doctrine in the exact sense of the word at any rate of method, and for errors which are positively harmful to the spiritual life. Two examples of this error of method are to be found in the way in which the essence of the spiritual life has so often been rendered complex and theories on the mystical life have failed to assign an adequate place to the Holy Eucharist.

There is surely no saint in modern times who has gone further than St. Thérèse of the Child Jesus in detachment from the means which lead to sanctity. For her "the divine lift [elevator]" is no mere metaphor, it expresses a perfect conception of simplicity. Just as once we have entered a lift we pay no further heed to the steps of the stairway but merely to remaining safely within the elevator, so in the "little way" of St. Thérèse we are no longer concerned about the ground we have covered, that is to say, we are not anxious to know at what stage of the spiritual life we have arrived and into what state of prayer we have entered, for our sole care is to remain within the divine arms. Our whole attention is directed so that we do not fall back, but maintain a constant surrender to Our Blessed Lord by humility, confidence and a generous love.

St. Thérèse could not read those books where "perfection is put before us with the goal obstructed by a thousand obstacles." The soul is often discouraged by such reading, and wonders when it will reach the end of so many trials. For St. Thérèse there are no barriers before God. At whatever stage of the spiritual life the soul may be, whether still struggling against sin or advancing in the practice of virtue, there is but one thing to do: "to surrender oneself more and more like a child to God's affectionate embrace" by repentance, confidence and love. To love without any thought for self, such is the wonderful simplicity of St. Thérèse. The soul which treads her "little way" has no other task than to seek that most precious simplicity of a little child, who has no other understanding than to love his Heavenly Father.

Thus, understandably Holy Communion was the great inspiration of St. Thérèse's simple, wholehearted life of love. Her First Communion was one of the peaks of her spiritual life. Let us recall this stirring passage from the Bull of Canonization:

"As soon as she had tasted of the Eucharistic Bread, she felt an insatiable hunger for that Heavenly Food, and, as if inspired, she begged of Jesus, her sole delight, to 'change for her into bitterness all human consolation.' Then, all aflame with love for Christ and His Church, she had a most keen desire to enter among the Discalced Carmelites, so that by her self-denial and continual sacrifices 'she might bring help to priests and missionaries and the entire Church,' and might gain innumerable souls for Jesus Christ. At the approach of death she promised that when with God she would continue this work." Thus we see all the intensity of little Thérèse's love for God, already so great, still further increased by her First Communion, and it would seem that this First Communion was the starting-point of her apostolic life and her devotion to the sanctification of priests.

From her earliest years it was her chief delight to talk frequently of God, and she always kept before her mind the thought that she must not inflict the slightest pain on the Holy Child Jesus. Notwithstanding this early union with God St. Thérèse had an ardent longing to receive the Eucharist. Holy Communion was not only a participation in the life of Jesus but the coming into her soul of Our Blessed Lord Himself. "How lovely it was," she says, "that first kiss of Jesus in my heart . . it was truly a kiss of love. I knew that I was loved, and said 'I love You, and I give myself to You for ever.' Jesus asked for nothing, He claimed no sacrifice. Long before that He and little Thérèse had seen and understood one another well, but on that day it was more than a meeting; it was a complete fusion." It was a veritable personal presence that she felt: ". . . Jesus alone remained the Master and the King." And we see Thérèse throughout her life yearning for this Heavenly Bread which she longed to receive daily.

In the world of today, as in the time of Pius X, there is an urgent need to learn this lesson. Many books on the mystical life omit altogether or assign only a very secondary place to the part played by Holy Communion in its development. It would appear that progress in the life of prayer is alone necessary in order to attain to intimate, experimental and finally habitual union with God. Union with God in contemplation becomes the essential aim to the detriment of Eucharistic union.*

If we had a deeper realization that the Holy Eucharist is more than a participation in grace, that it is indeed a participation in the very substance of God made Man we would unite ourselves more and more perfectly with Jesus in the Sacred Host; and in the simplicity of the life of faith, without any illusions our union with Him would often become a "fusion." Here we have the precise teaching of Pope Pius X, but it is also the teaching of all Catholic tradition from apostolic times. No wonder then that she who recalls us to the practice of the first centuries of the Church is named by the Pope of Frequent Communion "the greatest saint of modern times."

It would be difficult to utter a more sublime sentence than this, for it expresses in the simplest terms the reality of the most perfect love of God in complete detachment from the highest gifts of this life, gifts which derive from the experiential knowledge of the divine. The desire to await eternal life in order to know God other than in the night of faith is one of the most profound dispositions of St. Thérèse' soul. At no moment of her life does she depart from it, not even when her most ardent desire is fulfilled and she becomes united to her Divine Spouse in the Holy Eucharist. "I desire Him to come for His own pleasure," she confides, "not for mine."

It was the great simplicity of Our Lord's interior life as it stands out in the Gospel which attracted her above all else. "When I picture the Holy Family," she said, "the thought that does me most good is the simplicity of their home-life. Since Jesus has gone to Heaven now, I can only follow the traces He has left behind. But how bright these traces are! How fragrant and divine! I have only to glance at the Gospels; at once the fragrance from the life of Jesus reaches me, and I know which way to run; to the lowest, not the highest place! Leaving the Pharisee to push himself forward, I pray humbly like the Publican, but full of confi-

---

*This may have been the problem at the time that this article was originally written several decades ago, but now there is such a diminution of prayer and the spiritual life that some might be tempted to a certain quietism which is contrary to the Gospel, sound theology and above all to Thérèse's simple but very demanding method of love. That love is the perfect antidote to the subjective introspection of modern times which artificially divorces the exercises of prayer from their ultimate goal - Our Eucharistic Lord.

dence. Yet most of all I follow the example of Mary Magdalene, my heart captivated by her astonishing, or rather, loving audacity, which so won the Heart of Jesus."

In the simplicity of Our Lord's life St. Thérèse found the model upon which she would mold her own life right up to the end: "The death of love which I desire is that of Jesus on the Cross." And privileges which in His life on earth Our Lord had not chosen for Himself seemed to her of no value in her union with Him. The union of love, that alone was her goal: "Jesus! I would so love Him! Love Him as He has never yet been loved!"

We know that she reached this goal, for she herself tells us how she did it. "The only way to make quick progress along the path of divine love is to remain always very little. That is what I have done, and now I can sing with our holy Father, St. John of the Cross:

'By stooping so low, so low,
I mounted so high, so high,
That I was able to reach my goal.'"

Transforming union, *living communion with Christ,* was indeed the ideal to which she aspired throughout her life, and this aspiration derived from her great love for Our Lord. Transforming union seemed to her the only means of rendering Him love for love and responding in the most perfect way possible to His union with us in the Holy Eucharist. At the very beginning, on the day of her First Communion, grace had prompted her to cry: "I felt that I was loved and I said: 'I love You, and I give myself to You for ever.'"

"O Jesus, let me tell You that Your love goes as far as folly! In face of such folly, what can You expect, save that my heart should fly out to You? How can my confidence know any bounds? I know that the saints have done foolish things as well as wonderful ones, and my foolishness lies in hoping that Your love accepts me as a victim; it lies in counting on the angels and saints to help me, my beloved Eagle, 'to fly to You on Your own wings'.... Love calls to love, and mine longs to fill the abyss of Yours in its flight to You, but it is not even a drop of dew lost in that sea. If I am to love You as You love me, I must borrow Your love; I can find peace no other way."

She is conscious of having experimental knowledge of the divine truths and of Our Lord who contains them all, and she describes her mystical experience as follows: "Jesus has no need of books or doctors to instruct our soul. He, the Doctor of doctors, teaches us without the sound of words. I have never heard Him speak, and yet I know He is within my soul. Every moment He is guiding and inspiring me, and just at the moment I need them, 'lights' till then unseen are granted me. Most often it is not at prayer that they come but while I go about my daily duties."

This action of Our Lord in St. Thérèse as guide and inspirer is so strong, so predominant, that she attributed to Him all her virtue, all her sanctity, all her charity. "I know," she says, "that whenever I am charitable, it is Jesus alone who is acting through me, and that the more closely I unite myself to Him, the more I will be able to love all my Sisters." She expects no reward for her works because she has none of her own, but, she hastens to add," He will reward me according to His own works."

And so we see "little Thérèse" arrived at transforming union, in habitual "fusion" with Jesus. "Little" in the pejorative sense of the word for those who have not understood her way of absolute truth and simplicity, but for us ever greater and greater in proportion as we compare her life and teaching with the Gospel revelation of the life and teaching of Our Blessed Lord. The simplicity which Christ willed to establish in His relations with us provides the key to the spirituality of St. Thérèse of the Child Jesus. Too many of us forget the lesson which Our Lord gave to Philip when he asked to see the Father: " Philip, he that sees Me, sees the Father also." (Jn. 14:9). Our Heavenly Father is no less accessible than His Incarnate Son.

By becoming incarnate and giving us His Body for our daily Bread Our Blessed Lord has most surely willed to render easy for us the closest union with Himself. Before her First Communion she had already abandoned herself wholly and entirely to Our Lord in her simple way of love. Then, when Jesus came to her in the Holy Eucharist, He produced glorious fruits in her soul. Thérèse "had disappeared like a drop of water lost in the mighty ocean; Jesus alone remained the Master and the King."

In conclusion we would claim, then, that the genius of St. Thérèse of the Child Jesus lies in her simplification of the spiritual life and particularly in her return to the *simple eucharistic* spirit of the first centuries of the Church. It is not surprising, therefore, to hear a Pope of eminent sanctity declare her "the greatest saint of modern times," since that humble, rare simplicity which was hers received the unmistakable commendation of the Divine Master Himself: *"Whosoever therefore shall humble himself as this little child, he is the greater in the kingdom of Heaven."* (Mt. 18:4)

Editors Note: The above chapter is a condensation of an article, reprinted with with permission, from Sicut Parvuli. The original was heavily footnoted. To make it more easy reading we chose to drop the footnotes.

Saint Thérèse, Doctor of the Little Way

On October 20, 1997, St. Thérèse of the Child Jesus and the Holy Face joined two other women Saints in the ranks of the Doctors of the Church. Just twenty years ago St. Catherine of Siena and St. Theresa of Avila were proclaimed Doctors of the Church by Pope Paul VI shortly after the closing of Vatican Council II, which had opened up a greater role for the laity in the Church.

It is interesting to note that even as St. Thérèse prophesied that she would "spend her time in heaven doing good upon earth" so too a good case could be made, that even during her lifetime there were instances that pointed to the day when she would be declared a Doctor of the Church. They are found in her "Story of a Soul," one from the lips of St. Thérèse herself, when a small child, and the other, by her priest teacher when she was a eleven-year-old student in his religion class. Her father often took his favorite child, his little "Queen," on short excursions. On one occasion, returning home at night with her "king," she saw a cluster of stars that formed the letter "T." In her autobiography she writes, "I pointed them out to Papa and told him my name was written in the heavens." It is hardly a coincidence that in the Office of Morning Prayers for Doctors of the Church we read the following antiphon: ". . . Those who instruct the people in goodness will shine like the stars for all eternity."

At the Benedictine boarding school where she excelled in religion and science, but did poorly in mathematics and spelling, she showed great talent as a story teller and teacher. She loved to tell stories to her companions. Even the older girls were attracted to her stories which sometime ran over several days. "I liked to make it more interesting when I saw the impressions it produced and which were evident on my companions' faces. Soon the mistress forbade me to continue in my role as orator, for she preferred to see us playing and running and not discussing." She continues, "I grasped easily the meaning of things I was learning, . . . as far as the Catechism is concerned, I received permission to learn it during my recreation periods." She mastered the truths of the faith so well, often expressed in her own words, that her teacher, Father Domin, could always call on her to answer a hard question the other students could not; and as St. Thérèse relates in her autobiography, he "used to call me his *little doctor.*"

In the famous passage where she expresses her insatiable desire to be and do all things for the love she bore Jesus, she wrote: "Ah! in spite of my littleness, I would like to enlighten souls as did the Prophets and Doctors." It would seem that she left this option open when she said that "God does not inspire us with desires He does not intend to fulfill."

As a girl, Thérèse Martin, had a natural gift for teaching and in the Carmelite Order she was given the office of Assistant Novice Mistress. Coupled with this natural talent was an unquenchable thirst for the truth and knowledge. She points out in her autobiography that she could not count the number of books she read before she entered the Carmelites, none of which would impede her spiritual progress. Her favorite book in this period of her life was the "Imitation of Christ," which she read so often and used for meditation that she could recite from memory any part of it. However, what she was able to articulate as a young Carmelite Religious, in the "Story of a Soul" is explainable only through the action of Grace and her tremendous, heroic response to every Grace she received. In her own words, "I can not remember refusing God anything from the age of three."

She threw herself wholeheartedly into what ever she did. As a small child she and her sister, Céline, were offered a basket of toys and attractive things and were asked to choose whatever they wanted. After Céline had chosen a ball of wool, Thérèse was given the opportunity to choose. After a moment's reflection, she writes: "I stretched out mine saying: 'I choose all.'" She recalls that incident of her childhood as a summary of her whole life. "Later on when perfection was set before me, I understood that to become a saint one had to suffer much, seek out always the most perfect thing to do, and forget self." She understood that God offers many different opportunities to make sacrifice, many different degrees of personal holiness for each individual soul.

"Then, as in the days of my childhood, I cried out: My God 'I choose all!' I don't want to be a saint by halves, I'm not afraid to suffer for You, I fear only one thing: to keep my own will: so take it, for 'I choose all' that you will!'" When she embraced religious life she didn't settle for half measure. She had to become a great Saint; anything less than that would not do. With a sharp intellect, a phenomenal memory, an unquenchable thirst for the truth and the action of the Holy Spirit, one would expect great things of this ardent religious. She never disappointed those fellow religious who really understood her, accepted her wise counsels and were inspired by her heroic living the truth she professed so boldly.

There was no indication at the time of her canonization that she would ever be considered to be a Doctor of the Church, for at the time there were no women "Doctors." Yet her spiritual classic, the "Story of a Soul" with its universal, timeless, scriptural simplicity had and will ever have such a profound influence in the lives of countless twentieth century Christians, on into the twenty-first century, that it is comparable to the tremendous spiritual and social revolution introduced by the "Little Poor Man of Assisi" in the thirteenth century.

So how would St. Thérèse view this unexpected honor? Ever motivated by an uncompromising, unswerving quest for the truth, she readily admits that if the supreme Master-teacher found one more little and more abandoned to His merciful love than herself that person would have been chosen by Jesus to give the world her spiritual "Little Way." As the Church approaches the new millennium, St. Thérèse of the Child Jesus and the Holy Face joins the ranks of the illustrious Doctors of the Church, but always remaining as she so ardently desired, "the Heart" of the Mystical Body, there to love and teach others the science of love of Him who is Love.

—*The Editor*

Returning home one night with her Papa, little Thérèse saw a cluster of stars forming a "T." She pointed them out and cried to her father, "My name is written in the heavens!" Less than a century later, whenever her remains (relics) were publicly venerated, large crowds came to honor the Saint.

The Ordinary Life of a Spiritual Genius

Fr. Eugene McCaffrey, O.C.D.

Thérèse Martin was born in Alençon January 2, 1873, the ninth child (of whom five survived) of Louis and Zélie Martin. Both parents had tried unsuccessfully to enter the religious life and both longed undisguisedly that their children be dedicated to God in the priesthood or the religious life. Louis, a gentle, shy man, was a successful watchmaker, while Zélie, of much more lively and enterprising disposition, supplemented the family resources by making Alençon lace.

The Martin family and their immediate circle of friends belonged to a very specialized milieu, that of a Catholic France that refused to accept the secularization of the Church and had, in a sense, turned its back on the modern world. The whole religious atmosphere of the Martin family was characterized by an unquestioning obedience and loyalty to the Church, a strict ethical code and a Christian contempt for the world. The household was organized along almost monastic lines and the devotional life modeled on the acceptance of a patterned style of holiness. Nevertheless, within this self-contained and protected atmosphere, there existed a real and heroic goodness and a spirit of tender love and security.

During the first fifteen years of her life Thérèse was surrounded by this warm and devoted love and all the affection and acceptance to make her "the little queen" of the family. Though she was later to transcend and, in a sense, revolutionize her childhood spirituality, yet she was eternally indebted to it for it gave her the fundamental human experience of love, acceptance and security that become the basis of her unlimited trust in God.

Thérèse herself, in her *Story of a Soul*, divides her own early life into three distinct periods: the first four years of a happy and unruffled infancy before her mother died; the years from 1877-1886, her "winter of trial" when, as she said, her "strength of soul vanished" and she was plagued by extreme sensitivity, anxiety and recurring scruples — all of which, no doubt, was aggravated by her unhappy school experiences,

The house in Alençon where the Saint was born and witnessed her mother's death.

Pauline's entry into Carmel and her own mysterious illness; the third, from 1886 till her entry into the convent, starting with what she called her "conversion" — her "night of grace" — a grace that ultimately blossomed into the spiritual freedom and the heroic sanctity of her Little Way: "Charity took possession of my heart, making me forget myself, and I have been happy ever since."

The two years leading to her entry into the convent were for Thérèse a period of intense spiritual growth; the horizons of her soul expanded as "God," she says, "lifted me out of my narrow world." She experienced a growing conviction of the power of prayer — Pranzini, the famous criminal, scheduled to be executed, became the "first child," of her prayer — and an ever-deepening urgency to respond to the call to serve God and the Church in the religious life. With her new found freedom of heart, Thérèse's old gaiety and joy returned: "I was strong again and full of courage." She needed all her strength and all her courage to overcome the obstacles placed in her way. But she persevered; Thérèse was a fighter and God's grace was at work: "The divine call was so urgent that even if it meant going through fire, I would have cast myself in to follow Him."

In April 1888, at the age of fifteen, Thérèse entered the Carmelite convent of Lisieux — God's Ark, as she called it — and it was here she was to spend the remaining nine years of her life. Though it was for her, as she said, "the fulfillment of my dream," she also realized it was only the beginning — though even she herself could hardly have been aware of the still great and terrible challenge of the road that lay ahead.

The outward framework of her life in the convent is easily enough described. Early the following year she received the habit and the name "Thérèse of the Child Jesus." A month later her father suffered a stroke from which he never fully recovered and his ensuing mental illness was to be a vital factor in her own spiritual development. In September 1890 Thérèse made her Profession, adding to her religious name "the Holy Face," a title that was to become increasingly important to her. During her years in the convent she was employed in the normal range of domestic duties, alternating between refectorian, sacristan and portress, while at the same time helping with the everyday chores in the laundry, kitchen and garden.

When Thérèse was only twenty, her sister Pauline (Mother Agnes) was elected prioress and one of her first assignments was to appoint her younger sister as "Assistant Novice Mistress." Shortly afterwards Monsieur Martin died, ending five long years of what Thérèse called a "veritable martyrdom." Yet, for all that, she is adamant: "To me they were the most desirable and fruitful years and I would not exchange them for the most sublime ecstasies." A few months later, Céline — now relieved of her devoted care of her father — joined her three sisters in the convent. Later that same year, 1894, Thérèse, under obedience, began writing down the memories and recollections of her childhood which form the first part of *Story of a Soul*.

On Good Friday, 1896, Thérèse coughed blood, the first manifestation of the consumption that led rapidly to her death. In June of the following year, at the request of the new prioress, Mother Marie de Gonzague, she wrote the second part of her autobiography. The following month she was transferred to the infirmary and received the last Sacraments. But the slow and painful process of dying lasted until September 30. On October 4 she was buried in the town cemetery of Lisieux.

Such, in outline, are the facts and dates in the life of St. Thérèse of Lisieux. But behind these outward events lies another story — that of her soul. The story of a human being, a saint of God, who made the greatest journey of all, the journey towards heroic charity and the fullness of the Christian life. A saint who, forging her own way to God, mapped out a path for others to follow and impressed her own creative genius on a fresh and original expression of the Christian message.

—From "Christ to the World" with permission

Part II

St. Thérèse's Use of Scripture

By Msgr. T. Bird

In reading the Autobiography of St. Thérèse, "The Story of a Soul," one is struck by the number of scriptural passages that are contained therein. It is in this more than anything else that the authenticity and authority of her "Little Way of Spiritual Childhood" rests and is based. The following is a condensation of an article that first appeared in the magazine Sicut Parvuli by a scriptural scholar, the late Msgr. T. Bird, who was Professor of Scripture at Oscott College in England. Although St. Thérèse had no formal training in scripture, the author points out: "It is quite obvious she was guided from heaven in her use of the Sacred Books."

The Autobiography is not a big book, yet it contains more than 130 quotations from the Bible, besides a number of allusions. When we remember that St. Thérèse died at an age when most candidates for the priesthood have not yet left the seminary, and that during her religious life her time was fully occupied, until an illness (which usually gives the sufferer little taste for reading) confined her to bed, we are utterly astonished at her wonderful familiarity with both the Old and New Testament.

It is clear that she studied the whole Bible—Old Testament as well as New. In the Autobiography there are quotations from no less than thirteen books of the Old Testament (I, II, III Kings, Tobias, Psalms, Proverbs, Canticles, Ecclesiastes, Wisdom, Isaias, Ezekiel, Jonas and Joel). From the New Testament passages are drawn chiefly from the Gospels, but there are quotations from seven of the Epistles. The Psalms in the Old Testament and St. Luke's Gospel in the New seem to have been her favorite books. Yet up to the time of her entry into Carmel, she had not read the Scriptures. When she did discover the treasure she used it whenever she needed consolation during her trials and anxieties, or when she required an inspired guarantee for her teaching. Here are the passages:

"In my helplessness, the holy Scriptures and the Imitation are of the greatest assistance; I find in them a hidden manna, pure and genuine. It is from the Gospels, however, that I derive most help in time of prayer; I find in their pages all that my poor soul needs, and I am always discovering there new lights and hidden mysterious meanings."

"**Her teaching not only conforms to Scripture and the Catholic Faith, but excels for** *the depth and wise synthesis it achieved.* **Thérèse offers a mature synthesis of Christian spirituality:. . .She combines theology and the spiritual Life and expresses herself with strength and authority.**

—*From Pope John Paul's Apostolic Letter* Divini Amoris Scientia .

Pope John Paul with Bishop Guy Gaucher, author of the Preface and authority on St. Thérèse.

"I sought to find in holy Scripture some suggestion of what this desired elevator might be, and I came across these words, uttered by Eternal Wisdom Itself: *Whosoever is a little one, let him come to Me. . .* But wishing to know further what He would do to the little one, I continued my search, and this is what I found: *You shall be carried at the breasts and upon the knees; as one whom a mother caresseth, so will I comfort you.*"

"I draw from the rich mine which our Saviour has opened up to us in the Gospels; I search the depths of His adorable words, and I cry out with the Psalmist: *I have run in the way of Thy commandments since thou hast enlarged my heart.*"

"These aspirations becoming a real martydom, I one day sought relief in the Epistles of St. Paul, and my eyes lighted on the twelfth and thirteenth chapters of the First Epistle to the Corinthians. Straightway I was inspired to take up the Gospels and opening the book at random, I lighted upon a passage which had hitherto escaped me: *He whom God hath sent, speaketh the words of God, for God does not give the Spirit by measure.*

It is quite obvious that she was guided from heaven in her use of the sacred Book; she was "inspired" to consult it, and straightway she found the appropriate text. There is nothing here of the Protestant presumption of "private interpretation"; that would simply have horrified her. She loved Holy Church and its teachings with an ardent love; she would have

21

laid down her life in defense of any article of Catholic faith. "I am a child of Holy Church," she joyously exclaimed; and as a child of Holy Church she studied the sacred archives of the Church under the direction of the Church's teaching, but with special assistance from above.

Hence it is that in spite of the fact that she had never taken a course of biblical lessons she knew the Church's teaching on biblical matters with astonishing accuracy. She knew that the sacred Books were divinely inspired and that they were free from error; she studied the literal and historical sense first of all, but she did not stop there; she went on to "discover new lights and hidden mysterious meanings." Thereby she followed the method of the best exponents of the sacred text. We can almost hear her saying with St. Jerome: "I will tell you how you are to walk in the holy Scriptures. Everything that we read in the sacred Books shines and glitters even in the outer shell; but the marrow is sweeter. He who desires to eat the kernel must first break the shell. *Open Thou my eyes, says David, and I will consider the wondrous things of Thy law.*"

It would appear to me that her heavenly guide in her Scripture reading was no other than the Blessed Virgin Mary herself. Mary, who knew the holy writ so well, Mary, the ultimate author of the first two chapters of the third Gospel, Mary, who wrote in her mind all that happened to her Child and pondered over every detail, this same Mary seems to have been appointed by God as the patroness and teacher of all those saintly men and women who, in successive ages, have been raised up by the Holy Spirit in the Church to find their delight in the law of the Lord, to meditate on it, and then expound it for the edification of the faithful.

It would take us out of our way to develop this argument; we can only say that a long list of names beginning with St. Irenaeus of Lyons (who taught that Mary is the second Eve), and including St. Ephrem of Syria (who wrote Mary's praises in prose and verse), St. Ambrose of Milan, St. Jerome (the defender of Our Lady's perpetual virginity) and many others, down to Pere Marie-Joseph Lagrange, O.P. (in our own day), could be drawn up to illustrate its truth. It is not surprising then that when, under obedience, St. Thérèse of Lisieux was about to write the story of her soul she first knelt down before the miraculous statue of Our Lady to ask that her hand might be guided, and that at once that hand reached out to the book of the Gospels, where she read the words: *Jesus going into a mountain called unto Him whom He would Himself.* By those words "a clear light" was thrown upon the mystery of her vocation and of her entire life, "and above all upon the favors our Lord has granted to my soul." Mary was her tutor, and under her direction she learned the holy Scriptures with ever-increasing love.

Appropriate texts and passages seem to have come before her eyes in a marvelous manner. She fingered no concordance; she did not hunt through the pages of pious writers; nothing was borrowed from sermons or retreat exercises; she knew the Scriptures so easily that the right quotations simply flowed from her pen with a facility that is quite difficult to understand if we seek for merely natural explanations. The number of uncommon or out-of-the-way texts which she quotes is also surprising. Let us take a few and see if the reader can give the references:

"He gave us His kiss and now no one may despise us. . . .Man seeth those things that appear, but the Lord beholdeth the heart. . . .Tell the just man that all is well. . . .A net is set in vain before the eyes of them that have wings. . . .And therefore I have raised thee, that I may show My power in thee, and My name may be spoken of throughout all the earth. . . .A brother that is helped by a brother is like a strong city. . . .Yea, it is the Lord who hath bidden him say all these things. . . . I cry like a young swallow."

These are not hackneyed texts borrowed from pious manuals. They find their place in the Autobiography simply because its author was saturated with the dew of the divine Scriptures. It need hardly be said that the whole of St. Thérèse's teaching on spiritual childhood is founded on inspired passages of holy writ. Childhood supposes a father; St. Thérèse has proclaimed to the world that God is OUR FATHER. On one occasion, a novice entering her cell was struck by the heavenly expression of her countenance. Though sewing most industriously she seemed lost in contemplation. "What are you thinking of?" the young sister asked. "I am meditating on the Our Father," Thérèse replied, "It is so sweet to call God 'Our Father'!". . . and tears glistened in her eyes. As a natural foundation for the building up of this teaching God had given her a most lovable and saintly father, Louis Martin. From her earthly papa Thérèse turned her thoughts to her heavenly Father.

In the Old Testament the concept of God as a Father is unknown, except in a restricted and national sense. One passage only approaches the revelation of the New Testament, viz. Psalm 102, 13: *As a father hath compassion on his children, so hath the Lord compassion on them that fear Him;* but even here "they that fear him" are pious Isreaelites, children of the Covenant. It was Christ who taught us that God is the Father of all mankind because He made them all and loves them all. Yet, strangely enough, St. Thérèse after learning this great truth from the New Testament, found passages in the Old Testament that illustrated it. Speaking of the way of self-surrender she describes it as "the confidence of the little child who sleeps without fear in its father's arms," and as "quickly taking refuge in our Lord's arms, imitating those babes who when frightened hide their faces on their father's shoulder"; then her four proofs *ex sacra scriptura* for her teaching are all taken from the Old Testament.

1. From Proverbs 9,4: "Whosoever is a little one, let him come to Me."
2. From Wisdom 6,4: "To him that is little, mercy is granted."
3. From Isaias 40,11: "He shall feed His flock like a shepherd: He shall gather together the lambs with His arm, and shall take them up into His bosom."
4. From Isaias 66,12-13: "You shall be carried at the breasts, and upon the knees they shall caress you; as one whom a mother caresseth, so will I comfort you."

Thus was revealed to this little Saint the meaning of texts which 'wise and prudent' commentators had failed altogether to penetrate. "Because I was small and frail He deigned to stoop down to me and instruct me gently in the secrets of His love."

In these days St. Thérèse teaches us what the Greatest Doctor taught: "Love the Bible and wisdom will love you; love it, and it will keep you safe; honour it, and it will embrace you. . . Read assiduously and learn as much as you can; let sleep find you holding your Bible." For it was from the sacred Scriptures that St. Thérèse came to know our Lord so well. "Ignorance of the Bible means ignorance of Christ," says St. Jerome; and the converse is just as true, for, as Lacordaire puts it, "The Gospel is Jesus Christ living." Hence it is that in an age when the Church is calling upon her children to read the sacred Scriptures with greater diligence, St. Thérèse of Lisieux stands before us as a modern disciple of the great St. Jerome.

Thérèse had a natural brilliance, in spite of the fact that she was not very adept at either spelling or French grammar. Her supernatural insights were not only revealed in her prodigious grasp of the scope of Sacred Scripture and in her ability to apply individual passages and concepts to her own spiritual journey, but also in the facility with which she helped others, especially her novices, to see their own spiritual state reflected in the inspired text. Her gifts are also revealed in her relentless rejection of the allegorical interpretation of Scripture so common in her time but rather her pursuit of the literal sense of every text, and finally in her perfectly orthodox and organic integration of Catholic Tradition and Scripture in her spiritual teaching. All of this points to the fact that Thérèse, in a long line of saints and doctors, was and is, indeed, a "master of the Sacred Page." — *Fr. Frederick L. Miller*

The Real Thérèse Is Elusive

By Fr. Eugene McCaffrey, O.C.D.

For millions St. Thérèse of Lisieux has become an inspiration and a challenge. *Story of a Soul,* already in its fortieth French edition, has over fifty translations, making Lisieux as famous as the Eiffel Tower and giving to the Christian world a whole new vocabulary and a renewed school of spirituality.

Though famous, she is not always understood; though millions know her, not everyone has grasped her essential greatness and originality. She has had a bad press, and too often has been presented in cheap sentimental terms or, at the other extreme, as an unreal, superhuman model of virtue and innocence. It must be admitted, the real Thérèse is elusive; the limitation of her own stylized language, the cultural milieu in which she wrote, as well as her own love of hiddenness, make it essential that we probe beneath the image and strip the statue clean. Just how elusive Thérèse was, even to her own sisters in Carmel, is delightfully captured for us in one of the most vivid portraits we possess of her, written by Sister Marie of the Angels when Thérèse was twenty:

". . .tall and robust, with a childlike face, and with a tone of voice and expression that hide a wisdom, a perfection and a perspicacity of a woman of fifty. . . a little innocent thing to whom you would give communion without previous confession, but whose head is filled with tricks to be played on anyone she pleases. A mystic, a comedian, she is everything! She can make you shed tears of devotion, and just as easily make you split your sides with laughter during recreation." Hardly enough to make her "the greatest saint of modern times," but enough, surely, to make us cautious of any oversimplification about her.

Thérèse claimed that her life was a very ordinary one. Others were of the same opinion. "Whatever will Mother say about her?" one of the community wondered shortly before Thérèse died. Externally all this is true and the biographical details of her life are easily enough recorded (see page 155). Unknown to any of the great ones of her day, untouched by the political or social crises of the age, she lived nine of her short twenty-four years within the cloistered walls of a Carmelite convent. And yet, today, she holds her own with all her contemporaries, taking her place with the great thinkers and philosophers of her age, one who wrestled with the deepest problems of human existence, the enigma of human suffering and the ultimate question of life itself. With them she shared the suffering, the mystery and even the despair but not the ultimate solution; that was uniquely her own.

Monsignor Vernon Johnson, the great apostle of the Little Way, loved to tell the story of the old priest who, on the day St. Thérèse was canonized, turned to his colleague on the steps of St. Peter's and said, "It is the Gospel that has been canonized today." It would be difficult to express more accurately the whole life and message of St. Thérèse of Lisieux. To understand her is to understand the Gospel. Essentially her doctrine is nothing but a fresh and vigorous restatement of the basic Christian truths. This, in fact, was the genius of St. Thérèse that she rediscovered for her own age and for ours the hidden face of God. And she did so like an explorer, through the sheer force of her love and her burning desire to know the true heart of God. Without realizing it, she was giving back to the Church and to the modern world the God of the Gospels.

The heart of St. Thérèse's discovery was that the God of Revelation was a God of love and mercy. For her the "good news" of the Gospel was summed up in John's cryptic phrase "God is Love." The meaning of the Incarnation, as she understood it, was to make love visible. In her soul she experienced, in their deepest theological sense, Jesus' words from the cross, "I thirst," as a cry, a plea for the free gift of each human heart. For her He was a "beggar in love." She realized it did not matter how weak, fragile, even sinful these hearts were previously, as long as they were given in love. Hence her joy at the so-called "Gospel love scenes": the woman at the well, the good thief, Mary Magdalene. . . where love and mercy met and overlapped.

Where, for the majority of people, the truth of God's love is marginal, for Thérèse it was a truth to be lived, a central dynamic principle of her life. Her greatness was not that she discovered God's love but that she lived it at white heat. Fearlessly she stood before the abyss of God and the abyss of herself and found in the mystery of God's love for her the bridge — "the lift" as she called it — to reconcile them both. It is only in this way that we can understand the intensity of her inner life — her heroic virtue, her willing obedience, her patient acceptance of her father's humiliating illness, her daily faithfulness, and her gentle surrender to her own painful death. In the burning intensity of her love, old religious clichés — victim, sacrifice, abandonment, oblation — are given back their original beauty; they are purified and renewed. Her last words

"...tall and robust, with a childlike face, and with a tone of voice and expression that hide a wisdom, a perfection and a perspicacity of a woman of fifty... a little innocent thing... but whose head is filled with tricks to be played on anyone she pleases. A mystic, a comedian, she is everything! She can make you shed tears of devotion, and just as easily make you split your sides with laughter during recreation." —*Sr. Marie of the Angels*

"My God I love you," give meaning to her whole life and every particular detail of it.

Her life was love lived. Nothing was too small or too insignificant to be a vehicle of this love. She simply lived each day fully, never missing an opportunity to make this love visible: "a smile, for instance, or a kindly word, when I would rather say nothing or look cross." It was not the greatness of life that Thérèse discovered, but the greatness of the ordinary, the mundane, the trivial. The black and white dreariness of every day living was the raw material out of which she fashioned her "Little Way." For Thérèse there was no tomorrow; only today, lived out moment by moment in love. "Everything," she exclaimed, "is a grace." And when she said "everything" she meant everything.

On her death bed, the very day in fact that she died, Thérèse could sum up her life for her sisters with the statement: "I have never sought anything but the truth." A few weeks earlier she had expressed her understanding of truth in her ardent prayer; "O God, I beg you, answer me when I humbly say 'what is truth?' - Let me see things as they are, let nothing blind me to it." Seeing things as they are — this for Thérèse was the absolute condition of her way of spiritual childhood. To her search for love she brought a similar quest for truth, making her own St. Paul's summary of the Christian life "doing the truth in love."

Seeing things as they were was not easy for Thérèse. Her bold, independent spirit amazed and sometimes shocked her sisters. To one, taken aback by the directness of her answer, she replied, "If you don't want the truth, don't ask me questions." It was not so much that she rejected the devotional and the pious but that she purified and restored them to their true place in the Christian life. To her prayer, her devotion to the Blessed Sacrament, her love for our blessed Lady, her daily practice of virtue, she brought a realism and an authenticity that feared nothing except illusions. And, from illusions, she felt, "God in his mercy has always preserved me." In the last few months of her life, the honesty with which she confronted her own desolation of body and soul — the humiliation of her physical suffering, the darkness of her night of faith — proved too much for many of the community even to watch. Yet Thérèse could not dissimulate; "if I did not have faith I should have killed myself without a moment's hesitation."

Thérèse was not afraid of the truth; for her it was never hurtful or diminishing. On the contrary it was the essential condition for that true freedom of spirit which she so strongly desired. The truth, she knew, would make her free; free above all to be herself without any masks or any pretense before God or before others. Countless witnesses attest to her gaiety and spontaneity at recreation — "clever, witty and full of fun" one sister remarked, recalling Thérèse's impersonations and her ability to make others laugh. Again, how often her famous smile lightened the burden of another sister's weariness. Neither was she afraid to weep or show her emotions or admit defeat. She was the enemy of sham and of false virtue. A novice who boasted of her mortification in not eating her dessert was sent straight back to the kitchen to collect it! The infirmarian who asked her to say "something nice" to the doctor got an even more direct response, "let him think what he likes, I love simplicity, I hate humbug."

In her Little Way there was no room for theatricals and mock heroics. She was a saint who was not a hero; she loved her poverty, her weakness and her littleness too much for that. "We carry the cross," she told her novices, "not bravely but weakly." Seeing things as they are meant, above all, seeing herself as she was, accepting the full reality of her fragile humanity. The ingredients of her Little Way were the commonplace experiences of every human life: weariness, sadness, defeat, fear and disappointment. What for so many are stumbling blocks, for

Thérèse became stepping-stones. She knew that weakness was perfected by grace, poverty enriched by love. Hence her joy at coming before God "with empty hands" for it was only when they were empty that God could and would fill them.

When Mother Agnes was asked at the official Process of Canonization why she wanted to see her sister canonized, she replied spontaneously, "Because it will be for the glory of God, by proclaiming his mercy." In her constant striving to "do the truth in love" St. Thérèse discovered there was ultimately only one thing that made it all possible: the mercy of God.

Thérèse starts her Autobiography with the words, "I am only going to do one thing: start singing now what I must repeat forever: the mercies of the Lord." She ends the same story of her soul by saying, "I do not know how this story will end, but what I do know is that the mercy of God will accompany it forever." And to her sister Marie she could say, "What pleases God most is the blind hope I have in His mercy. This is my only treasure."

The climax of Thérèse's life was the self-offering to Merciful Love that she made in June 1895. Quite on her own, without guide or teacher, save only the Spirit living in her heart, she came to discover the core of revelation "that the mercy of the Lord is above all his works."

For Thérèse, ever practical and daring, there had been only one response, to launch out full sail on the way of confidence and trust. Where others opposed mercy and love, Thérèse in the simplicity of her childlike vision saw them both as one. Henceforth she would not speak of one or the other but only of the totality: Merciful Love.

Once Thérèse grasped this new found vision of God she never looked back. She took God at his word and surrendered herself totally to Him. She offered everything and God, for His part, accepted the offering. Many things she let go herself willingly — her natural affection for her own sisters, the human props and comforts that the self so eagerly craves — but there were many things that God asked of her in darkness and in faith. He led her into the deeper trials of the spirit, where her soul was cleansed and purified in what she could only describe as a "night of nonexistence" and where she mingled with the mocking spirits of atheism and unbelief.

Yet her confidence held firm and she pushed trust to the limit: "Even if God kills me, I will still trust in Him." Even when the very foundation of her confidence was removed — her "vision" of heaven, her idea of God, her certainty of His love — she still trusted. And in one of her most extraordinary phrases, reminiscent of the great Teresa of

Avila, she shows the stubborn determination of which the saints are made, "He will get tired of making me wait for Him long before I get tired of waiting for Him!"

And so Thérèse had come the full circle. She had set out on her journey to God with boundless desires. "I choose all," she exclaimed in her childhood enthusiasm, "no use in becoming a saint by halves." But, in the end, she had to let everything go: nothing was to remain but God. She made the longest and the greatest journey of all and, in doing so, opened up a path — a way of spiritual childhood — to make the Gospel message as fresh and clear as on the first Easter morning. The last sentence in the last letter she ever wrote told it all, "He is love and mercy — that is all!" In her own fearless quest for truth and love Thérèse had touched the core of every human spirit where the whole fragile world of men and women meets. She found strength in weakness, victory in defeat, life in death. She had released the human spirit and set holiness free.　　　　　*—Reprinted with permission of Christ to the World*

Left: the cell of Sr. Thérèse. Right: stairs to her cell

"The cry of Jesus on the Cross: "I thirst!" resounded continually in my heart. These words made me burn with a zeal which I had never experienced before. . . I wanted to answer the appeal of my Beloved and I myself was consumed by the same thirst for souls. . . It was not now those of priests that preoccupied me but those of great sinners. I was aflame with the desire to snatch these souls from eternal fire." (Saint Thérèse of the Child Jesus: "Story of a Soul")

Humility and Truth *Versus* Intellectual Pride

The following two part chapter contrasts St. Thérèse with three con-temporary French writers who have done much harm to the Church in our times. This chapter which deals more with the dissenters and mod-ernists than with St. Thérèse (she is amply covered in the rest of the book) highlights her virtue of heroic Faith as lived in total obedience to her superiors and loyalty to the Magisterium of the Church.

The first part by the eminent theologian, Fr. John Hardon, is taken from the article *St. Thérèse of Lisieux,* which appeared in "The Catholic Faith Magazine" of September/October, 1997.

THIS YEAR IS the centennial of the death of St. Thérèse of Lisieux. It comes almost on the eve of the twenty-first century. We can safely say that never before in Christian history has there been more need for an unhappy world, intoxicated with self-love, to learn from her that the only true happiness comes from surrendering one's heart to the Heart of God.

If we look closer at St. Thérèse's importance for our times, it be-comes even more clear as we see the virus of pride infecting so many people in our day. As the popes are at pains to explain, whatever else the modern world needs, it is a rediscovery of the meaning of Christ's teach-ing about becoming like little children. He could not have been more solemn than when He warned us, "Amen I say to you, unless you turn and become like little children, you will not enter into the kingdom of heaven" (Matthew 18:3). This injunction was always necessary, but it is crucial today when human achievements in the material world have intoxicated millions with self-conceit and widespread oblivion of God.

Unlike the great Catholic books of history, the Autobiography of St. Thérèse of Lisieux hardly has a historical setting that occasioned its publica-tion or shaped its composition. Its author lived only twenty-four years, and nine of those were spent in the obscurity of a Carmelite cloister.

Yet there is a deep sense in which we can speak of the historical circumstances in which the book was written. Two French writers, who were contemporaries of St. Thérèse, give us some insight into the devastating ideas that began to plague Christianity in her day. Ernest Renan, the ex-seminarian of Brittany, repudiated the divinity of Christ, portrayed Him as a charming Galilean preacher, and denied that He had ever worked any miracles. Alfred Loisy, a priest from Lorraine, denied that Christ ever founded a Church or instituted any of the sacraments.

No contrast could be more startling than to compare, for example, Renan's *Life of Jesus* or Loisy's *Gospel and the Church,* with the Autobiography of St. Thérèse. She is writing in a spirit of deep faith, especially faith in the Divinity of Christ; time and again she speaks to Jesus, as "My God"; whereas Renan and Loisy abandoned the faith they once had; and then studiously contradicted what they had formerly believed.

What should be emphasized, however, is that St. Thérèse's faith was severely tested. An essential part of her sanctity, therefore, was her courageous profession of faith in spite of the serious temptations against the faith that God allowed her to experience.

The latest publication of Thérèse's sayings reveals this side of her life which many commentators have overlooked. She was not only plagued with trials about the faith, but she saw the sufferings that God sent her as a providential means of obtaining or restoring faith for unbelievers. "I offer up," she confided to her superior, "these very great pains to obtain the light of faith for poor unbelievers, for all those who separate themselves from the Church beliefs."

Keeping this in mind will give an entirely new dimension to St. Thérèse's practice of spiritual childhood. She was an extraordinarily gifted person, with a penetrating intellect. Yet she believed and grew in the faith almost because her faith was so sorely tried by the Lord.

Fr. Teilhard's Studied Ambiguity and St. Thérèse's Simplicity

ANOTHER STUDY, by Fr. Patrick O'Connell, pointing to the contrast between St. Thérèse and the modernist approach to the Catholic Faith appeared in the June-July, 1971 issue of the IMMACULATA magazine. Father O'Connell wrote a rebuttle to an article that favorably compared St. Thérèse with Fr. Teilhard de Chardin based on two quotations taken from their writings. In a letter to her Sister Céline, Thérèse writes: "The older we become the more we love Jesus and it is in Him that we love one another." The phrase from Fr. Teilhard's *Divine Milieu* reads: "Without the existence of a Supreme Center of Convergence, men can never love one another mutually." It is hardly possible to see a close similarity of two contemporaries from one isolated quotation from each.

When this article appeared Teilhard's writings were very popular in Catholic intellectual circles. Though his popularity has declined his influence is still being felt. The quoted passages do not indicate necessarily a simliarity between the two. In fact they give us a clue of what to expect in reading the two contemporary authors. St. Thrérèse uses simple language a child can understand. Whereas Fr. Teilhard is quite ambiguous, seemingly purposely so. The reader may read whatever he wants in the terminology which Teilhard "invents." But a true comparison has to take into consideration the lives and thoughts express in their writings.

Father O'Connell, a St. Columban Missionary, who spent twenty-three years in China as a missionary, during the 23 years that Teilhard was there, pointed out that the French Jesuit wasn't there to win converts, but to pursue his research in the origin of the human race (Paleontology). St. Thérèse never left her monastery for a foreign land to win souls for Christ; yet her desire to win souls motivated her to live a life of heroic prayer and penance. So great was her desire to win souls, she promised before her early death to help the missionatries from heaven. She was so successful in keeping her promise that she has been named co-patroness of the missions.

Though both were religious, born and raised in France in the later part of the nineteenth century, their conception of religious obedience were totally dissimilar. The traditional understanding of the religious vow they both took, seemed to escape Teilhard. His sense of obedience fits in well with the dissenters of our day. Perhaps that explains his popularity with those who take exception to what Rome and the Holy Father teach.

The Columban Missionary priest points out, that his writings were proscribed by the Holy See, first by Pope Pius XI then by Pope Pius XII for espousing the condemned theory of polygenism and again by subsequent Popes and religious superiors. Contrary to his vow of obedience, since his superiors forbade him to publish his manuscripts, he ensured their publication after his death, by giving them to literary executors who included prominent atheists. On the other hand we see in a number of chapters in this book how exacting the obedience of St. Thérèse was. She would not be a canonized Saint were it otherwise.

The writings of Fr. Teilhard were examined by the Holy See and his Jesuit superiors and both agreed they were not fit to be published because they contained grave errors against the Faith. The Holy Office under Pope Pius XII issued a decree in 1957 ordering his works removed from seminary libraries and Catholic book stores. The same Holy Office under

Pope John XXIII issued a solemn warning, called *Monitum*, June 30, 1962 against his writings and declared that they contained grave errors and were a serious danger to the Faith. The present Pope confirmed that warning in 1981 shortly after the assassination attempt on his life. In spite of all this, many seminarians and theologians lionized Teilhard, some even thinking he would some day become a Doctor of the Church. Like so many works inspired and motivated by intellectual pride rather than obedience to the Will of God, these writings will eventually be consigned to the dust bin of history. As St. Paul points out, everyman's works will be tried by fire, and nothing but ashes will remain of Teilhard's works

The opposite is true of St. Thérèse. Without any pretense of writing something that would be earth-shaking, and which was written only under holy obedience, she composed a spiritual classic that will endure to the end of time. Today, she is rightly recognized as a Doctor of the Church. The three requirments for being named a Doctor were easily fullfilled: a holiness that is outstanding even among other canonized saints; the depth of her doctrinal teachings; and the extensive body of writings which the Church can recommend to her members as being free from error and fathful to her authentic tradition.

Had more religious and priests acquired the humility and simplicity of a little child by reading the *Story of a Soul* and applied its wise teachings in their lives, we would not be experiencing today's vocation crisis.

—The Editor

First Confession of St. Thérèse

When recounting her first sacramental confession, Thérèse writes: "Well instructed in all I had to say and do, I entered the confessional and knelt down. On opening the grating Father Ducellier saw no one. I was so little my head was below the arm-rest. He told me to stand up. Obeying instantly, I stood and faced him directly in order to see him perfectly, and I made my confession like a *big girl* and received his blessing with *great devotion* for you had told me that at the moment he gave me absolution the *tears of Jesus* were going to purify my soul. I remember the first exhortation directed to me. <u>Father encouraged me to be devout to the Blessed Virgin and I promised myself to redouble my tenderness for her.</u> (emphasis added) Coming out of the confessional I was so happy and light-hearted that I had never felt so much joy in my soul. Since then I've gone to confession on all the great feasts, and it was truly a *feast* for me each time."

— From *Story of a Soul*

Heroic Parents — Models for Our Times

Mary Ann Budnik

St. John Vianney believed "If a child goes to hell because of the neglect of his parents to teach him his faith, you can be sure the parents will follow." If this is true, then surely the converse is also true, as we see in the example of the Martin family. St. Thérèse achieved the exalted position of Doctor of the Church by drawing on the spiritual formation she received from her devout parents, Louis and Zelie Guerin Martin, and her elder sisters Pauline and Marie. As proof that "God gave me [Thérèse] a father and a mother more worthy of heaven than of earth," her parents have been declared Venerable. Imitating the example of the Martin family we can raise *our* children to be saints.

Zelie Marie Guerin, the mother of St. Thérèse, was the second of three children. While her family history was one of staunch faithfulness to the Catholic faith even in times of cruel persecution, her young life was not easy: "My childhood and youth were shrouded in sadness; our mother did not know how to treat me, so I suffered deeply." Still, the faith and pious practices taught in her home led both her and her sister Marie-Louise to seek religious vocations. Her sister, upon entering the Visitation convent at Le Mans, told the superior, "I have come here to be a saint!" Isidore, their brother, became a pharmacist, and eventually settled in Lisieux.

When Zelie asked for permission to enter the Daughters of Charity she was told by the superior that it was not the will of God that she become a religious. Disappointed, she prayed: "Lord, since, unlike my sister, I am not worthy to be your bride, I will enter the married state in order to fulfill Your holy will. I beg of You to give me many children and to let them all be consecrated to You." God answered her prayer by sending her Louis Martin for her husband and nine children, of which five daughters survived to become consecrated religious.

While Zelie waited for God to arrange her marriage she prayed to Our Lady for direction as to her uncertain future. December 8, 1851, she received her answer in the form of an interior locution: "See to the

The Saint at age 3 1/2. Her mother wrote of her, " She is very intelligent but not nearly so sweet a disposition as her sister and her stubbornness is almost unconquerable." Mother and child, painting by her sister, Céline.

making of Pont d'Alençon lace." She immediately entered a lace-making school, quickly mastering the intricate art in order to begin her own business which proved successful and lucrative. It was here also that she met her future mother-in-law, Marie-Anne Martin, who immediately decided that Zelie would be the perfect wife for her son Louis.

Louis Martin, Thérèse's father, was one of five children. His father, like Zelie's, was a soldier, not only of France but also of Christ. When his regimental chaplain remarked how long he knelt after the consecration of the Mass he explained: "It is because I believe!" The faith of Louis' mother is also evident from her letter to him: "Dear son, I think of you when my soul, upraised to God, follows my heart's longing, and soars to the foot of His throne!"

Louis, besides being a handsome man, was well-read, witty and cultured. He enjoyed gardening, hunting, fishing, socializing and singing. Gifted with artistic skills, he decided upon a clock and watchmaking career. While apprenticed in Strasburg, he saved the son of his father's friend from drowning but was unable to bring this lax Catholic family back to the faith. He felt they were "pursuing their earthly way without casting a thought to what awaits them at the end."

Louis sought to enter the monastery of the Great St. Bernard but the prior told him to first learn Latin and then re-apply. After a year and a half of unsuccessful private tutoring in Latin, Louis resumed his career as a clock and watchmaker and later as a jeweler. This time he studied his craft in Paris. There Louis was approached to join a "philanthropic club" which turned out to be a branch of freemasonry. Louis, indignant over the deception of his friends, refused to join. Another time a group of his friends decided to have a seance. At first he refused to take part because of the demonic element involved. He finally agreed to be a passive spectator, all the while praying that if the demonic was involved the attempt would fail, which it did.

Louis had a reputation of doing everything with patience, order, neatness and precision. His tedious and precise work he did well, offering it to God. Proof of his skillfulness is in the fact that his watches were still running long after his death. Although absorbed by his profession, he set strict priorities: God first and everything else in the proper order. On Sundays his shop was closed in order to keep holy the Sabbath. He neither bought nor sold on Sunday although this cost him business. Zelie believed that Louis' prosperity was linked to his strict observance of Sunday: "I can only attribute the easy circumstances he enjoys to a special blessing, the reward of his faithful observance of Sunday." Out of a sense of justice, he paid his bills and salaries promptly. He never lived beyond his means.

St. Thérèse at the age of twelve when she broke the news to her Father that she wanted to join her two sisters in the Carmelite monastery of Lisieux. On hearing this unexpected news the father didn't discourage his youngest daughter from entering the Carmelites but looked upon all his daughters entering religious life as a gift from God.

Crossing the bridge of Saint Leonard, Zelie passed a distinguished looking young man. Glancing at him, she heard interiorly: "This is he whom I have prepared for you." Introduced shortly thereafter, the couple were married three months later on July 13, 1858. Louis was thirty-five and Zelie was twenty-seven years old. The first ten months of their marriage, the couple lived as brother and sister until a confessor intervened. In the next fifteen years nine children were born, seven girls and two boys of which only five daughters survived. Children were valued by the Martins. Mme. Martin, a prolific letter writer, wrote: ". . . for me, my children were my great compensation, so that I wished to have many in order to bring them up for Heaven." The couple longed for sons who would become priests and daughters who would become religious. At the birth of each child, Zelie consecrated the child to God saying: "Lord, grant me the grace that she may be consecrated to You, and that nothing may ever come to tarnish the purity of her soul. If ever she is to lose it, I prefer that You take her at once."

The Martins realized that each of their children was a child of God, a temporary gift He had given them to form in faith and virtue. They did not dream of earthly success for their children. Instead, the Martins focused on sanctity for their children. While Zelie did not live long enough to see her dream realized, Louis knew the joy and pain of offering his daughters as Brides of Christ. Marie writes about his reaction when she asked permission to join Pauline in the Carmelites: "He stifled a sob and said brokenly: "Ah! Ah!. . .But without you! The good God could not have asked a greater sacrifice of me! I thought that you would never leave me!" When his "little Queen" asked to join the Carmel by her fifteenth birthday, he not only took her to the Bishop so that she could personally ask for early admittance but also took Thérèse to church saying: "Come, let us go together to the Blessed Sacrament to thank the Lord for the graces he bestowed on our family, and for the honor He gave me of choosing His spouses in my home. Yes, if I possessed anything better, I would hasten to offer it to Him." Twelve days after Thérèse received the Carmelite habit, he was hospitalized for a mental illness from which he would never fully recover. He truly became "a living sacrifice." To a doctor he confided: "But I know why God has given me this trial. I have never had any humiliation in my life; I needed one."

As a sign of the couple's devotion to the Blessed Virgin, each child was given the name of Marie irregardless of sex, as had been the custom in the Guerin family. The first son would have the secondary name of Joseph. To avoid confusion, the children were called by their secondary patrons except for the eldest daughter who was called Marie. No secular names for the Martin family! They wanted patron saints for their children for protection as well as an example for their children to emulate. Each child was baptized either on the day of birth or the day after, no later. They did not wish to risk a child dying without first becoming a child of God as Zelie related in a letter to her brother: "Whatever you say, we shall have another child. But if God wills once more to take this one from me, I pray that it may not die unbaptized, so that at least I may have the comfort of three little angels in Heaven."

Abandonment to the will of God was the cornerstone of the Martin family. The crosses and sufferings which the family endured with each child's death only served to deepen the parents' faith. Announcing the death of her son Marie-Joseph, she wrote: "My dear little Joseph died in my arms at 7 o'clock this morning. I was alone with him." Upon his death she cried out, "Oh, God, must I put that in the ground! But, since You will it, may Your will be done." When she became pregnant with her next child she wrote to her sister-in-law: "You could not imagine how I fear for the future as regards the little one I am expecting. I feel as though the fate of the last two will be its fate also. I think the dread is worse than the misfortune. It is a continual nightmare for me. When the sorrows come, I resign myself fairly well, but fear is a torture to me. During Mass this morning my thoughts were so gloomy that I was thoroughly upset. The best course is to leave everything in God's hands, and await events in calm and *abandon* to His will. That is what I am going to make myself do."

Suffering was not easy for Zelie: "Oh dear! How tired I am of suffering! I have not a grain of courage left. I am impatient with everybody. I often say during the day: My God, how I long to be a saint!' and then I do not labor to become one!"

Despite their great sorrows, the Martin marriage was a happy one. Louis gave Zelie the freedom to manage all the domestic and housekeeping affairs. She in turn called Louis a "saintly man" who made her "always very happy." She told her sister that Louis "made [her] life very sweet." When her lace-making business became too large for her to handle alone, Louis sold his own business and took over the management and sales for Zelie. Although married, Zelie and Louis consecrated their lives to God by becoming members of the Third Order of St. Francis.

Besides their family, both Louis and Zelie had their businesses to run. Madame Martin writes: "It is so sweet to attend to little children. If I had only that to do, I think I should be the happiest of women. But their father and I must work to earn enough for their dowries, otherwise when they are grown up they will not be pleased."

Mr. Martin with his two daughters,
Céline (left), Léonie (right).

According to the testimony of Pauline, their second daughter, "In spite of her hardworking life, mother attended half-past five Mass every morning with father, and they both went to Holy Communion four or five times a week. Towards the end of his life father became a daily communicant." As the children grew up, they accompanied their parents to daily Mass. After their thanksgiving after Holy Mass, the Martins returned home to breakfast and morning prayers with their daughters. On the way home from Mass Mr. Martin would not join his daughters conversation. Instead he told them, "You will excuse me, children, for I am continuing my conversation with the Lord." Even when Zelie was near death from breast cancer, she would struggle to get to Sunday and First Friday Masses, almost passing out before reaching the church doors.

The custom of morning prayers before the statue of Our Lady of the Smile with the parents present was an important part of each day. When Zelie was dying Thérèse and Céline spent the day at a friend's home. Thérèse, only four at the time, later wrote: "Céline whispered to me on the way home: 'Ought we tell her we haven't said our prayers?' I said yes, and she explained to Madame Leriche, who replied: 'Never mind, you'll say them now,' and went off, leaving us together in one of the big rooms. Céline looked at me and we both agreed: 'Mamma would never have done that. She always made sure we got our prayers said.'" Thérèse related later that as a little girl, "I loved God very much and I offered my heart to Him very often, making use of the little formula that mother had taught me."

Mr. Martin's devotion to the Blessed Sacrament was demonstrated by his frequent holy hours and Nocturnal Adoration. Each day Thérèse and her father would take a walk that would lead them to a different church for a visit to the Blessed Sacrament. Not bothered by human respect, he always tipped his hat when passing a church, and would kneel down in the street when the Blessed Sacrament passed by in procession. He even removed the hat of a man who sneered as the monstrance passed. It was Louis who made sure that anyone dying in the neighborhood had a priest present to give the last sacraments.

Charity toward the poor and suffering was an ongoing concern of the family. During Thérèse's daily walks with her father, she was given money to disperse to the needy they met along the way. On Monday evenings beggars gathered at the gate of their home. It was Thérèse who

The saint and Céline, Thérèse's boon companion. Though the younger Thérèse entered before her sister who took care of their father in his final illness, it was Thérèse who prayed and convinced her older sister to enter the Carmelites.

was given the task of dispersing alms to them. Her mother, despite long days spent with her business and family, would spend hours at night nursing sick neighbors, and helping poor families with money, food and clothing. Orphans and widows also received help as well as businessmen in financial straits.

Concern for souls was uppermost in the minds of this family. Zelie, concerned about her brother living in Paris, beseeched him to avoid temptations by praying: "I beg of you, dear Isidore, to pray, and you will not let yourself be carried along with the stream. If once you give in, you will be lost. It is only the first step that costs, on the way of evil as on that of good. After that you will be borne along by the current. You live close to *Our Lady of Victories.* Go in, just once a day, to say an *Ave Maria* to her. You will see that she will protect you in a quite particular way." To her sister-in-law she writes: "Under what illusion do the majority of men live! Do they possess money? Forthwith, they want honors. And when they obtain these, they are still discontented, for the heart that seeks anything but God is never satisfied." She confides to her brother: "Prosperity draws men away from God. Never does He lead His chosen by that road; they must first pass through the crucible of suffering in order to be purified."

The Martins were a fun loving family. Their evenings were spent talking and laughing together. Mr. Martin would play checkers with his daughters or teach them folk songs. Sometimes Zelie would play cards with her daughters and then have to stay up late to finish her sewing. There were also readings of general interest or some carefully screened novel along with poems. Secular newspapers were banned from the home for Louis wanted his daughters educated in Christian truth, not the ways of the world. The Martin girls were avid readers and each had her own copy of *The Imitation of Christ.* As young children, the girls could quote passages verbatim. At evening prayers, Thérèse knelt next to her father: "I had but to look at Papa to learn how the saints prayed."

Through family interaction, Louis would teach them lessons. He made a set of weighted cones that Thérèse could knock down but would spring back up. He pointed out to her that, "In the trials and shocks of life, you must rise up again after every fall and keep looking up!" On one of their walks, Thérèse's puppy jumped into a pond then rolled in the dirt, getting his white and brown fur filthy. Louis used this illustration to teach his daughter about sin: "See, that reminds us of a spotless, white soul which becomes soiled by sin." Although busy, Louis made time to give a daily spiritual talk to his daughters.

The Martin girls were taught to make little sacrifices (mortifications) to the Child Jesus so that they could add "pearls" to their crowns in heaven. Marie recalls her first mortification at the age of four or five years old. She had asked her father to make her a saucer out of her orange peel. When she showed it to Pauline "it made you envious and, *to have a pearl in my crown* (that was the way mother used to make us do things) I gave it to you. It seemed to me that I was accomplishing an heroic act, because that famous orange skin seemed all the more precious to me because you wanted it. Then, running quickly towards mother, I said: 'Mama, if I gave my orange skin to Pauline, will I go to heaven?' Mother smiled and answered: 'Yes, my little daughter, you will go to Heaven.' That hope alone was able to console me for the loss of *my fortune.*"

When Grandfather Guerin died, nine-year-old Marie faced the dentist bravely hoping to get her grandfather out of Purgatory. When it came time for little Thérèse to make her First Communion her sister Pauline, now a Carmelite, asked Thérèse to prepare for receiving Jesus by making little acts of sacrifices and love. Thérèse recorded 818 little acts of sacrifice and 2,773 aspirations of love.

While the five daughters were affectionately and lovingly raised, the parents were not permissive. At the Process of Beatification her daughters reported: "We were not spoiled. Our mother watched very carefully over her children's souls, and not the smallest fault ever went unreproved. Her training was kind and loving, but attentive and thorough." Once a parent made a decision, it was law. Zelie writes: "Do not be uneasy if your little Jeanne has a temper. I remember that until the age of two Pauline was the same. I must tell you, however, that I never spoiled her and, little though she was, I never let anything pass unchecked. Without making a martyr of her, I nevertheless made her obey." If arguments arose, Louis would simply have to say "Peace, children, peace!" to restore order to the home. Céline recalled that: "Never did I hear one of us at home say one disrespectful word to our parents, not even an off-hand one. We never questioned an order received; it never even occurred to anyone. We obeyed from love."

Meals were not prepared according to the different tastes of the girls. They were expected to eat what was placed in front of them. The Martin girls were also schooled in the various human virtues by their parents. They were to be polite, courteous, humble, clean, orderly and punctual. Vulgar language was not permitted. When her daughters attended social activities Mrs. Martin enjoyed having her daughters attractively dressed. When her sister, Sister Marie-Dosithee protested, Zelie replied, "Must they shut themselves up in a cloister? In the world we cannot live in seclusion!" After Mass on Sundays the family would picnic in the country and then returned to church later in the day for Vespers. They observed the feast days and fast days strictly and took part in retreats and pilgrimages.

Mrs. Martin suffered from breast cancer for twelve years. When medication failed to arrest the cancer, she and her three oldest daughters made a pilgrimage to Lourdes to beg Our Lady for a cure. When she was not cured she wrote: "What do you want? If the Holy Virgin does not cure me, it is because my time is done and the good Lord wants me to rest someplace other than the earth."

Upon her death, Marie and Pauline, well trained by their parents, successfully undertook the formation of their younger sisters. Fr. Stephane-Joseph Piat, O.F.M. writes in *The Story of a Family:* "Normally, the saint receives his early fashioning in the home circle." We have seen how this was done in the life of the Little Flower. The question we must consider is how are we forming our own children in the light of eternity? As St. Augustine exhorts us: "Cannot I do what these men and women did?"

The Martins were a close knit and happy family, which endured many tragedies but were sustained by their deep Catholic Faith. **Right:** The famous *Les Buissonnets* home in Lisieux.

Part III

1. Abandonment Through Suffering

Msgr. Vernon Johnson

2. Counsels to Her Novices

Sr. Marie of the Trinity, O.C.D.

3. The Last Words of the Saint

Mother Agnes, O.C.D.

4. Devotion to the Holy Face

Fr. Frederick L. Miller

5. Restoring Missionary Zeal Where It Begins

Bro. Francis Mary Kalvelage, F.I.

Abandonment Through
Suffering

Msgr. Vernon Johnson

But what about suffering and sorrow and all the pain and evil of life? Has the Little Way any answer to this, the central tragedy of human existence? When the little soul finds that even pain and suffering are all within the heavenly Father's love, are all precious gifts from the heavenly Father to His child, by which that child is cradled in His arms more securely than by anything else, it knows then that nothing can hurt it. "Jesus was pleased to show me," St. Thérèse says, "the only path which leads to the divine love. This path is the abandonment of the little child who sleeps without fear in its Father's arms."

Some people have misunderstood this imagery and think that the little soul thus depicted rests inert and lifeless in the arms of God. But what the little child does by instinct in the natural sphere, the soul must do by grace in the supernatural. The sleep of the little child is the parable of that peace which comes from a completely surrendered will, a will entirely surrendered from moment to moment. This demands continual activity, an activity comparable with the activity of a drowning man who, suppressing his natural instinct to trust in his own efforts, in abandoning himself, entirely, to the man who swims to his rescue, an act demanding the highest courage and the most perfect self-control.

That this abandonment is an active thing is apparent every time St. Thérèse speaks of it. On the day of her Profession she prays: "I offer myself to Thee, O my Beloved, that Thou mayest perfectly accomplish in me Thy holy will." A few years later, writing to her sister, she says: "My desire is to do always the will of Jesus. Let us leave Him free to take and to give whatever He wills. Perfection consists in doing His will, surrendering ourselves wholly to Him. . . . The more content a soul is to accomplish His will, the more perfect it is."

"From my childhood these words of Job's delighted me: 'Though he kill me, yet will I trust in him.' But I confess it was long before I was established in this degree of abandonment. Now I am there. The Lord took me and placed me there." From this ceaseless activity issued her peace. "To suffer peacefully is not always to find consolation in the suffering, for peace is not always accompanied by joy, not at least by sensible joy. To suffer with peace it suffices that we truly will all that God wills."

From this we see, and it is most important that this should be understood, that the abandonment of the little soul is in no sense a gesture of despair, as the English word might lead us to suppose. It is, on the contrary, that act of reckless joy with which a little child flings itself into its mother's arms. Such is the philosophy of the little saint whom God has chosen to guide us by her Little Way. This abandonment of hers was tested to the uttermost in the terrible spiritual desolation which her heavenly Father allowed her to pass through during her last illness. How does she meet it? With the absolute simplicity of a little child.

In her suffering at the end of her life she reveals that it was this which gave her so much strength. "If I did not simply live from one moment to another it would be impossible for me to be patient, but I look only at the present. I forget the past and I take good care not to forestall the future. When we yield to discouragement or despair, it is usually because we think too much about the past or the future."

Nor is this all. The little soul is drawn into a deeper mystery still. As it suffers with Him, it shares not only in the pain of His Cross but in the redemptive power of that Cross; and its sufferings, in union with His, call down from Calvary graces upon other souls. Writing to her sister, St. Thérèse says: "Let us offer our sufferings to Jesus for the salvation of souls." In these simple words lies all the theology of St. Paul regarding the mutual sufferings of the Mystical Body, whereby the sufferings of one member avail for the succor of another member in virtue of their union with their common head. "I rejoice in my sufferings for you and fill up those things that are wanting of the sufferings of Christ, in my flesh, for his body which is the Church" (Col. 1: 24).

It was this secret — that her pain and suffering were the supreme means of union between her soul and our Blessed Lord, and were also the means of sharing in the redemptive work of His Cross — that made suffering and pain to her a most precious thing. "Far from complaining to Jesus of the cross that He sends us, I cannot fathom the infinite love that has led Him to treat us thus." "I thank Thee, O my God, for all the graces Thou hast bestowed on me, and particularly for having made me pass through the crucible of suffering."

So she passed along her Little Way smiling always and with a song of joy on her lips, "I will sing. I will always sing, even though I have to pluck my roses from amidst the thorns; and the sharper and the longer the thorns, the sweeter shall be my song," no mere words. For eighteen months she was the victim of tuberculosis in its most painful possible form. The doctor who attended her said: "If you only knew what she has to endure!

I have never seen anyone suffer so intensely with such a look of supernatural joy."

But, more even than this, her heavenly Father gave to her the further gift of spiritual desolation, which is so often the mark of His tender love for the saints. To her sister St. Thérèse describes this trial: "If you were to judge by the poems I have composed this year, it must seem as though I had been flooded with consolations, like a child for whom the veil of Faith has almost been rent asunder and yet it is not a veil, it is a wall which rises to the very heavens and shuts out the starry sky. When I sing of the happiness of Heaven and the eternal possession of God, I do not feel any joy therein, for I sing only of what I wish to believe."

The condition of all supernatural life is the complete dying to self and birth into love which is the work of Calvary in the individual soul. "Unless the grain of wheat falling into the ground die, itself remains alone. But if it die, it brings forth much fruit. He who loves his life shall lose it, and he who hates his life in this world keeps it unto life eternal' (Jn 12:24-25). It is the complete taking possession of the soul by the heavenly Father's love so that, emptied of self, it may be filled with that divine love, caught up into the divine love. The more completely the little soul is consumed by the divine love, the more it is transformed into the divine life of union with God through love.

Thus God crowns the abandonment of His little child: thus, abandonment makes all things sweet. And this is all worked out through just the little things of everyday life which the heavenly Father presents to us, His children, as little means of sacrifice whereby we may become complete victims of His love. In the Little Way of Spiritual Childhood the little soul does not ask for suffering, but gladly welcomes all that the Father gives. It is this complete abandonment of the little victim that shines out so wonderfully in the last illness of the Saint, and enabled her to bear indescribable pain with joy.

A few days before her death she said to her sister: "Do not be troubled if I suffer much and show no sign of peace at the end. Did not our Lord Himself die a victim of love, and see how great was His agony!" Almost her last words were: "Yes, all that I have written about my thirst for suffering is really true. I do not regret having surrendered myself to love." Then, looking at her crucifix, she said: "Oh, I love Him. My God . . . I love . . . Thee." These were her last words. Suddenly she raised herself, as though called by a mysterious voice, and opening her eyes, which shone with an unutterable happiness and peace, she surrendered her soul into her heavenly Father's arms, to the end His little child.

—*Excerpted from the booklet "Spiritual Childhood"*

Counsels to Her Novices

By Sr. Marie of the Trinity, O.C.D.

Sr. Marie of the Trinity, the favorite novice under St. Thérèse, gives us insights in the wisdom of the Saint far beyond the age of twenty, when she was placed over the novices. But more by her example she directed her novices to heroic sanctity. The following are excerpts from Sister Marie's testimony. She was one of fifteen persons who knew the Saint intimately. These testimonies were used in introducing her cause for beatification.

What people, even her own sisters, say about her now seems to me to fall short of what I saw in her. Since she was always correcting my faults, I would have liked to find some imperfection in her, but I never could. She never tried to win my affection by natural means and still she won it entirely. I felt that the more I loved her, the more I loved God too; when my love for her sometimes grew cool, I felt my love for God diminished too. I found that strange and could not understand it, until one day she gave me a picture, on the back of which she had written these words of St. John of the Cross: "When our love for another person is wholly spiritual and based on God alone, then as it grows the love of God in our souls grows with it."

I once asked her if Our Lord was displeased with me, seeing I was so imperfect. "Rest assured," she said, "that He whom you have taken as your spouse has all the perfections that one could desire, but, if I may say so, He has one great weakness: He is blind! And there is one branch of knowledge he is ignorant of — mathematics. . .no, His love for us makes Him positively blind!

"I believe in the [Little Way of trust and love] so firmly that if the pope himself were to tell me that you had been wrong, I think I would still believe in it," I once said to her She replied rather sharply "Oh! you should believe the Pope before anybody else, but don't be afraid that he is going to tell you to change; I won't give him time to. If, when I get to heaven, I find that I have deceived you, I will obtain permission from God to come back straight away and tell you. Till then believe that my way is safe and follow it faithfully."

She had a knack of using everything to stoke up the fire of love.

One day I spoke to her about magnetism, and the extraordinary things I had seen in this connection. The following day she said to me: "How I wish I could get myself magnetized by Jesus! How gladly would I have handed over my will to Him! I wish He would take possession of all my faculties, so that I could no longer perform personal, human actions but only deeds that were wholly divine — inspired and guided by the Spirit of Love."

In pointing out how one lady strayed from her Little Way, she said: "People must not think that our 'little way' is a restful one, full of sweetness and consolation. It's quite the opposite. To offer oneself as a victim to love is to offer oneself to suffering, because love lives only on sacrifice; if one is completely dedicated to loving, one must expect to be sacrificed unreservedly." Another time she said: "Before I entered Carmel, when I woke up in the morning I used to think about what the day might have in store for me, and if I foresaw annoying things I got up depressed. Now it's the opposite: the more opportunities I can foresee of bearing witness to my love of Jesus and of earning a living for my children, the poor sinners, the more joyful and courageous I am, and I tell Jesus: "Look, you worked and wept enough for thirty-three years here on earth; today you can take a rest, it's my turn to fight and suffer."

When the community worked together she would place herself next to the sisters who seemed downcast or depressed. Since she could not speak to them, she smiled affectionately at them and tried to be as obliging as possible. There used to be a sister (she has since left us) who had moods of the blackest depression. Nobody could ever work with her for long. Sister Thérèse took pity on this unhappy person and seeing a great opportunity for sacrificing herself more fully for God's sake, she asked Mother Prioress to let her help this sister in her work. I related to Sister Thérèse how I lost my patience with an elderly nun who had a temperament that would try the patience of a saint. She was also exasperatingly slow and very eccentric in her ways. She retorted that Sister Thérèse never spoke to her like that. Sister Thérèse said: "Be very gentle with her; she is not well. Besides, it's only charity to let her think she is rendering us a service, and it gives us an opportunity to practice patience. What if you had to listen to [a nun who tried everyones patience] as I have to do?" Sister Thérèse said to me. "Now you can do what I do. It's really very easy. All you have to do is to mellow your soul with charitable thoughts: you then feel such peace you no longer get irritated."

One day I asked her how she prepares for Holy Communion. She said: "I imagine my soul as a child with dirty clothes, and hair in disarray from playing. These misfortunes happen from doing battle with souls. But Our Lady immediately takes charge of me. She takes off my dirty smock, tidies my hair, and puts a pretty ribbon in it. That's enough to make me sufficiently pretty again to take part in the Angels' feast without embarrassment."

"If you are sick," she would say, "just tell Mother Prioress about it: then leave it to God, and don't worry about it, whether they give you proper treatment or not. You have done your duty by informing the prioress, and that is enough. The rest is not your business, but God's. If He permits you to lack something, that is a grace: it is because He is confident that you are strong enough to suffer something for His sake."

Once I saw Mother Agnes speak to another nun and place more trust in her. I complained to Sister Thérèse. To my surprise, she said: "You think you love Mother Prioress very much don't you?" "Of course I do," I replied, "Otherwise I wouldn't mind her showing preference for others." "All right. Now I'm going to prove that you are absolutely wrong. It is not Mother Prioress that you love; it is yourself. When you really love a person, you rejoice to see the beloved person happy. If you loved Mother Prioress for her own sake, you would be glad to see her finding some pleasure at your expense. Since you think she found you less pleasant to talk to than someone else, then you should not be hurt when you appear to have been passed over."

One day I wanted to omit mental prayer because of urgent work. She said: "Unless the necessity is very great, never ask to be dispensed from community exercises for the sake of work, no matter what it is. That kind of dedication cannot be pleasing to Jesus. Real dedication is to never waste a minute, and to give oneself fully during the hours set aside for work."

I once skillfully let the sister sitting next to me know that I had been forgotten when feast day desserts were served. Sister Thérèse overheard me and made me bring it to the attention of the sister who had served the desserts. I implored her not to make me do this, but she said: "No, that's your penance; you're not worthy of the sacrifice God asks of you. He asked you to do without dessert, because it was He who permitted you to be forgotten. He thought you generous, and you disappointed Him by drawing attention to the fact."

One day I was looking for a little appreciation for having behaved virtuously. She replied: "What's that compared to what He has a right to expect of you? You should rather be humbling yourself at the thought of all the opportunities for virtue that you have let slip by." Her retort was a salutary lesson; even now it stops me from being complacent when I do anything good.

The Servant of God's obedience was heroic. When Mother Gonzague was prioress she imposed a legion of petty regulations which she repealed or changed according to her fancy, with the result that little attention was paid to them. Sister Thérèse observed every one of them, and obliged me to do the same. She showed exemplary fidelity to the least commands.

Sister Thérèse would keep for her own use only what was strictly indispensable, and the uglier and poorer these were, the happier she was. She used to say that there was nothing sweeter than to lack what was necessary.

I once approached her in a matter of purity that bothered me. I told her, "I'm afraid you won't understand anything about my problems." She smiled and replied: "Do you think purity is a matter of being ignorant of evil? You needn't be afraid to tell me anything you want to; nothing will surprise me." After she had comforted me and restored my peace of soul, she made the admission: "There is only one thing I have not experienced, and that is what is called pleasure in this matter."

One elderly nun could not understand how so young a person as Sister Thérèse could be put in charge of the novices. At recreation one day she made no secret of her opposition. She said to Sister Thérèse that "She would be better off directing herself rather than others." I was watching at a distance. The Servant of God's angelic meekness contrasted strongly with the passion of the sister speaking to her, and I heard her answer: "Yes, sister, how right you are! Indeed, I'm much more imperfect than you think."

One day when I expressed a desire to be stronger and more energetic, in order to practice virtue better, she said: "If God wants you to be as weak and powerless as a child, do you think your merit will be any less for that? Resign yourself, to stumbling at every step. Love your powerlessness, and your soul will benefit more from it than if, aided by grace, you were to behave with enthusiastic heroism and fill your soul with self satisfaction and pride."

Seeing her so sick, I said to her one day: "How sad life is!" "But life is not sad," she replied. "If you had said 'the exile is sad,' I could understand. People make the mistake of calling what must come to an end 'life,' but it is only to heavenly things to what will never end, that one should really apply the word. And in this sense, life is not sad; it is blessed, very blessed." *St. Thérèse of Lisieux by Those Who Knew Her,* see ad on page 161.

The Last Words of the Saint

During the last months of Thérèse's life, Mother Agnes of Jesus (her sister Pauline) was given permission to be with her sister. As they conversed she jotted down her inspiring words. These last words portray a frail human being suffering intensely, but with such heroism, patience and at times even joy that it is incomprehensible apart from the grace of God. Seemingly abandoned by God and the Blessed Mother, she persevered to the end in her love for Jesus identifying with Jesus crucified in His seemingly abandonment by the Father.

—Editor

MAY 15, 1897

I no longer find anything in books, with the exception of the Gospel, that book is enough for me. . . . I do not mind if I live or die. I do not really see what more I shall have after death than I already have in life. It is true that I will see the Good Lord! But I am already completely with Him on earth.

When I think of these words of God: "My reward is with me, to render to each one according to his works (Apoc. 22:12)," I tell myself that He will be very much embarrassed in my case. I haven't any works! He will not be able to reward me "according to my works." Well, then, He will reward me "according to His works."

MAY 18

Since my duties were taken from me; I was thinking that my death would cause no disturbance in the community. . . . *I asked her: "Does it cause you any pain to pass as a useless member in the minds of the nuns?"* As far as I am concerned, it is the least of my worries; it makes no difference to me at all.

MAY 27

I always see the good side of things. . . . If I have nothing but pure suffering, if the heavens are black so that I see no break in the clouds, well, I make this my joy!

JUNE

It is certainly a great grace to receive the sacraments; but it is all right, too, when the Good Lord does not allow it — everything is a grace.

JUNE 13

Even if I had done everything Saint Paul did, I would still think myself a "useless servant," but it is precisely this that makes me happy for since I have nothing, God will give me everything.

JULY 21

What does it matter to me whether it is I or somebody else who shows this Little Way to others; provided it is shown, what does it matter who shows it! I ask you humbly, what is truth? Let me see things as they are, let nothing throw dust in my eyes.

JULY 30

She was hemorrhaging and choking for breath so bad we didn't expect her to survive the night. "It is dreadful to see you suffer so much, you must not be able to think." No, it still lets me tell God that I love Him. I think that is enough.

AUGUST 7

Oh how little God is loved on this earth, even by priests and religious! No, God isn't loved very much.

AUGUST 9

We told her she was a saint. No, I am not a saint; I have never done the works of a saint. I am a very little soul that God filled with His graces, this is what I am. What I tell you is the truth, you will see in heaven.

AUGUST 11

I often pray to the saints without receiving any answers; but the more deaf they are to my prayers, the more I love them. *I asked why?* Because I've had a great desire not to see God and the saints in this life and to remain in the night of faith, rather than like others who have desired to see and understand.

AUGUST 22

Oh little Mother, what would happen to me if God didn't give me courage? I have only the use of my hands now! We don't realize what it is to suffer like this. No, we must experience it.

AUGUST 25

Sister St. John of the Cross used to enter every evening, place herself at the foot of the bed and laugh at her for a long time. Yes. It is painful to be looked at and laughed at when one is suffering. But I think how Our Lord on the cross was looked at in the same way in the midst of His sufferings, and even worse they were really mocking Him.

SEPT. 11

I love you so very, very much! When I hear the door opening, I always think it is you; and, when you do not come, I am sad. Give me a kiss, a kiss that makes a noise, the kind of kiss you can hear!

SEPT. 30

I looked after her during morning Mass. She said nothing to me. She was exhausted, panting for breath. . . . Joining her hands for a moment, she looked at the statue of the Virgin and said: Oh! I have prayed to her with such fervor! But this is pure agony, with no trace of consolation. . . . O my dear Blessed Mother, help me. . . .My God, take pity on your poor little girl! Take pity on her, O my Mother, I tell you, the chalice is full to the brim! . . .but of course, the Good Lord will not abandon me. . .he has never let me down. . . .Yes, my Lord, anything You wish, but have mercy on Me! . . Yes, I think that I have never looked for anything but the truth. Yes, I have understood the heart's humility. . . I think that I am humble. . . everything I have written about wanting to suffer, oh, it is all true!. . . And I do not regret having given myself to Love.

See Bibliography *St. Thérèse of Lisieux: Her Last Conversations*, page 159.

The last photograph of the Saint taken exactly a month before she died.

Devotion to the Holy Face

Fr. Frederick L. Miller

Long before Scriptural scholars came to realize the immense Christological significance of the Servant Songs of the Deutero-Isaiah (Is 42:1-9; Is 49: 1-7; Is 50: 4-11; Is 52:13-Is 53), Thérèse of Lisieux had discovered them and placed them at the very center of her spirituality. These texts revealed to Thérèse the abandonment of Christ to the will of the Father in taking upon Himself the sins of the whole world. They, likewise, revealed to her His salvific love as the motive of His vicarious suffering for human sins.

These texts of Isaiah, discovered by Thérèse during her early years in Carmel, were to form the foundation of her devotion to the Holy Face of Jesus. It was precisely this devotion which allowed her to identify herself with Christ in the mystery of His suffering for others. The prophet Isaiah helped her in the midst of her own intense suffering, caused by her father's illness, to understand that it is possible not only to suffer for others but, through suffering, to bring them healing and salvation. In these passages, Thérèse began to grasp that her personal sufferings were an actual participation in the passion of Christ.

In this context she found great comfort in the contemplation of the Face of Jesus in His passion. In "Story of a Soul," Thérèse thanked Pauline for introducing her to this devotion. She noted that her devotion to the Holy Face had helped her to supernaturalize the intense sufferings she had experienced during her first years in the convent: "If only my face could be hidden away, like His, pass unrecognized by the world to suffer and to remain unnoticed, that was all I longed for." It must be underscored here that Thérèse's devotion to the Face of Christ was, in her mind, rooted firmly in the texts of the Suffering Servant of Yahweh in which she savored the mystery of co-redemption.

On January 10, 1889, when Thérèse was clothed in the habit of Carmel, she added the title "of the Holy Face" to her religious name. It should be observed that shortly after Thérèse's entrance, her father suffered his physical and mental breakdown. In the "Story of a Soul," Thérèse compared her father's suffering to the passion of Jesus. She also recog-

Thérèse and the Holy Face

The image on the Sacred Shroud of Turin discovered on a photographic negative for the first time just a year after Thérèse's death. She had a great love and devotion of the Holy Face of Jesus, which at that time was portrayed on Veronica's veil. In her own words, "If the Heart of Jesus is a the symbol of love, His adorable Face is its eloquent expression."

nized that his illness offered his daughters the opportunity to enter deeply into the paschal mystery of the Lord. Thérèse had felt very close to her father in his suffering. She wanted to help her sisters understand that this experience was permitted by God in order to unite them more closely to Christ in His passion. Many of her letters to Céline, during this period, centered on the Suffering Servant as the model of the Christian's vicarious suffering for others.

Céline, who was then preparing to enter Carmel, cared for her father during his final illness. On July 10, 1890, Thérèse wrote to her and sent her the text of Isaiah 53. She urged her sisters to recognize Christ's sufferings reflected in their own. She also suggested that Céline see the mercy of God in the cross that He had sent to their family. She wrote: "Jesus has sent us the best-chosen cross that He could devise in His immense love. . .How can we complain when He Himself was considered 'as one struck by God and afflicted.'"

As she was dying, Thérèse confided to Pauline the great part these texts had played in her spiritual life: "These words of Isaiah: Who has believed our report? There is no beauty in him, no comeliness, etc., have made the whole foundation of my devotion to the Holy Face, or, to express it better, the foundation of all my piety. I, too, decided to be without beauty, alone in treading the winepress, unknown to everyone."

These words are highly significant. In them Thérèse reveals that the Suffering Servant of Yahweh, i.e., Jesus in His "kenosis" bearing all human sins as if they were His own, had been the very foundation of her spiritual way. Thérèse intimates in this passage what she had explained frequently throughout her life to Mother Agnes: The suffering that she had experienced was at a level far deeper than her physical and mental agony and was, in a sense, ineffable. Thérèse believed that only in the next life would others understand the degree of her union with Christ in His passion. For instance on July 30, 1897, Thérèse, pointing to a glass containing a very distasteful medicine that looked like a red-currant liquor, said:

"This glass is an image of my whole life. Yesterday, Sister Thérèse of St. Augustine said: 'I hope you are drinking some good liquor!' I answered: 'Oh Sister Thérèse, it is the worst possible thing to drink!' Well, little mother, this is what happens in the eyes of creatures. It has always seemed to them I was drinking exquisite liquors and it was bitterness. But no! My life hasn't been bitter because I know how to turn all bitterness into something joyful and sweet."

In her spirituality, which had been firmly built upon the texts of Deutero-Isaiah, Christological and soteriological in content, Thérèse found the means of interpreting and sanctifying her many physical and spiritual trials. She also found in these texts the means of offering her sufferings in hidden union with Christ in His passion for others. Contemplating the Suffering Servant of Yahweh, stricken for the sins of His people, Thérèse realized that if she united her sufferings to the perfect self-offering of Christ, He would bring many souls to His Father through her.

The fourth song of the Suffering Servant became very important to Thérèse throughout all of her religious life, but especially in her final, and physical sufferings. In the words of the prophet applied properly, of course, only to the Messiah, but in an adapted and participatory sense to herself also, Thérèse grasped the full meaning of co-redemption:

"And yet ours were the sufferings he bore, ours the sorrows he carried. But we thought of him as someone punished, struck by God and brought low. Yet he was pierced through for our faults, crushed for our sins. On him lies a punishment that brings us peace and through his wounds we are healed" (Is 53:4-5). As in her name, St. Thérèse of the Child Jesus of the Holy Face, so also in her Scriptural spirituality, Jesus in His "kenosis" is central—Jesus the beloved Son always doing the Father's will; Jesus, rejected and crucified, bearing personally the guilt of human sin.

Exerpted from the Article *"St. Therese and the Word of God"* from the booklet *St. Thérèse of Lisieux: Doctor of the Church?* with permission of **Catholics United for the Faith.**

Restoring Missionary Zeal Where It Begins

By Bro. Francis Mary Kalvelage, F.I.

It is a paradox that St. Thérèse, chosen to be co-patron of the missions along with St. Francis Xavier, never left her convent in Lisieux from the time she entered at the age of fifteen until the day she died, September 30, 1897. This twenty-four year old Carmelite nun hidden away in an obscure corner of France is placed beside the great Jesuit apostle of the Indies as the patron saint of the missions. What a contradiction when men in our day look for visible, tangible and measurable accomplishments. Yet, without seeking honor or notoriety she is acclaimed as the greatest saint of the twentieth century, and hardly a Catholic Church is found without a statue of her (at least that was true thirty years ago).

All this fame came to her, not because she sought notoriety, but just the opposite. Paradoxically, she desired to be forgotten — as unnoticed as a grain of sand. Secondly, she was a woman of great desires, capable of great love. Thérèse knew that these desires were meant to be realized. She reasoned that God would not give her such great desires if He did not intend to fulfill them.

In one of the most lyrical and important sections of her autobiography she describes her insatiable desire to love Jesus as He had never been loved before. In order to please Jesus, and win salvation for many souls, she would be a warrior, priest, apostle, doctor of the Church and a martyr. She could not limit her vocation to just working in one mission station, but would "travel over the whole world to preach the gospel and plant His cross on infidel soil, but not for a few years only but from the beginning of creation until the consummation of the ages."

She wanted to be an "apostle of apostles," sharing in the apostolic labors of the missionaries, with her prayers and sacrifices. Not satisfied with sharing in their labors, successes and failures in this life alone, she promised to support them from heaven. Shortly before her death, she wrote one of the two missionary priests, whom she was given to share in their missionary work: "I will not be inactive in heaven, my desire is to continue working for the Church and souls. I ask this of the Good Lord and I am sure He will grant me this wish." Indeed, God has granted her wish, judging by the thousands of missionaries that have sought her help, and reaped a plentiful harvest of souls.

Her missionary spirit and role as "missionary supreme" needs to be emphasized more today than ever before. Our Lord's command, just before He ascended into heaven: "Go into the whole world and preach the Gospel to all men" (Mk 16:15) is being questioned. Karl Rahner's notion of "anonymous Christian," which plays down the whole idea of working strenuously for the conversion of pagans has infected even missionary Orders and Congregations in the Church. As a result, it is not considered of vital importance to expend so much time and zeal as in the past for the salvation of souls in the foreign missions. Pagans, according to the "anonymous Christian" interpretation of missiology, "already have grace but not . . .'the full Christian awareness.' Neither faith nor salvation depends on the help of the Church; God's salvific action precedes that of the Church; man is already saved." (see "Christ to the World" pg. 246, 1968). Then, why be concerned over the salvation of non-Christians as the Church has taught from its very beginnings? Why bother trying to convert them? St. Maximilian Kolbe, who promised to pray for the canonization of St. Thérèse if she would help him in his great missionary work in the Orient, gives the answer to that dangerous misconception: "The loss of a single soul is a great disaster."

The Saint clearly saw the distinction between the work of Christ in establishing the Church in the plan of salvation and the work that eventually procedes from that Church in which missionaries play a vital part in the salvation of souls. It is this distinction which the novel phrase "Anonymous Christian" tragically erases.

The following are some startling facts. Between 1921 and 1965, the years just before and immediately following her canonization saw the foundation of more than forty missionary congregations inspired to carry on Thérèse's mission of saving souls, especially souls that had never had the Gospel preached to them. Since then, due to a decline in missionary zeal, there have been less than eight such foundations.

Fortunately, the missionaries of the last century planted the seed of the Gospel well. What were mission countries then, today are countries that have their own seminaries sending missionaries to other countries. This is particularly true of Africa. The nineteenth century, when Thérèse lived her short life, saw great missionary expansion in every corner of the globe. Every major Catholic country had missionary societies forming

Shortly before her death St. Thérèse wrote her two missionary priests, "I will not be inactive in heaven, my desire is to continue working for the Church and souls. I ask this of the Good Lord and I am sure He will grant me this wish." Indeed, through the mediation of her immaculate Mother, Thérèse has let fall many graces to thousands of missionaries that have sought her help.

thousands of religious and priest volunteers for the missions. When Thérèse's sister, Céline, showed her a missionary journal, Thérèse refused to read it. The temptation to change her mind was too great. She had already decided to enter the Carmelites. Through much prayer of discernment she realized that she could do more in saving souls and spreading the Gospel as a contemplative, drawing down many graces through a hidden life of prayer and sacrifice, than if she were to follow the dictates of her heart. How right she was!

We see from the early life of St. Thérèse right up to her last days a continuous awareness and growth in the traditional missionary spirit. From external appearances, her early childhood and family life appeared to be typical of the comfortable upper middle class in France at that time. The bourgeoisie had retained a certain Catholic sense, which was perhaps more cultural than spiritual. But this was not so in the Martin family circle. Both of Thérèse's parents at first entertained the thought of a religious vocation. Through frequent and even daily attendance at Mass, reading of scripture and the lives of the Saints; and above all the example of an outstanding devout father (her mother died a holy death when Thérèse was only four) as well as the example of her sisters, Thérèse learned that love was synonymous with sacrifice. As a small child, she was taught by her sisters to make little sacrifices to please God and win the grace of conversion for sinners. The smallest and seemingly insignificant events of life could win souls for Christ. God's Merciful Love was revealed to her in an incident which occurred when she was thirteen years old:

"One Sunday, on closing my book at the end of Mass, a picture of the crucifixion slipped partly out, showing one of the Divine Hands, pierced and bleeding. An indescribable thrill, such as I had never before experienced, passed through me; my heart was torn with grief at the sight of the Precious Blood falling to the ground, with no one to treasure it as it fell. At once I resolved to remain continuously in spirit at the foot of the Cross, that I might receive the divine dew of salvation and pour it forth upon souls. . . .I was consumed with an insatiable thirst for souls, and I longed at any cost to snatch them from the everlasting flames of hell."

This craving for the salvation of souls was soon to be blessed with a most remarkable conversion. A notorious murderer, Pranzini, was condemned to death and, according to the newspaper accounts, he gave no sign of repentance. She offered prayer and sacrifice for the unfortunate man. She made bold to say: "My God, I am sure that you will pardon this unhappy Pranzini, and I shall still think so even if he does not confess his sins or give a sign of sorrow—such is the confidence I have in your unbounded mercy." But with childlike candor and feminine delicacy, she added that since this is her first sinner, she would like to have one sign of repentance to assure her that her prayers were answered. As he mounted the scaffold, under the prompting of grace, he turned to the priest standing nearby, seized the crucifix he held toward him and kissed Our Lord's Sacred Wounds three times. With this clear sign of the answer to her prayers and sacrifices, her zeal for the salvation of souls knew no bounds.

When she was only fourteen she wrote in a letter: "It is a joy to think that for each pain cheerfully borne we shall love God more for ever. Happy I would be if at the hour of my death I could offer Jesus a single soul. There would be one soul less in hell, and one more to bless God for all eternity." Once inside the Carmel, her loving embrace of suffering became a preoccupation. "Suffering opened wide her arms to me from the first and I took her fondly to my heart. . . .Our Lord had made me understand that it was through the Cross that He would give me souls, the more crosses I encountered the stronger became my attraction for suffering. . . ."

In her convent there were nuns who practiced greater austerities than did St. Thérèse. Due to her youth and frail health she could not engage in the extraordinary, so she made much of pouring every ounce of love into all the small insignificant events in life. Even her failures gave her an opportunity to humbly admit her nothingness and trust that much more on God's infinite mercy and love.

Toward the end of her life, she wrote of her great desire to involve many other souls as evangelizers. She even prophesied shortly before her death that God would raise up a whole "legion of victim souls" to follow in her footsteps, as victims of God's Merciful Love. This prediction was largely realized by means of her autobiography, "Story of a Soul" (see page 159). Her missionary zeal, which would involve the laity as well as religious and priests, anticipated Vatican II's decree on the laity in the Church's mission.

Everyone is called to be a missionary and the Church is continually on mission. As if to underline her untiring zeal of winning souls for Christ, through prayer and penance, Our Lady appeared in 1917 in Fatima, Portugal, exhorting her children, "To pray and make sacrifice, for many souls go to hell because there is no one to pray and make sacrifice for them." Catholics who follow her "little way" of heroic sacrifice by being faithful in the ordinary things in life in a spirit of reparation to the rejected love of God are thus fulfilling Our Lady's plea of participating in the salvation of souls.

Both by word and action Thérèse set the example. The hidden sacrifices which she strove to make to please Jesus may be summarized well in her own words: "I will let no sacrifice escape me, no look, no word, nor deed. I will make use of the smallest actions, and I will do them for love." Continuous fidelity, to the day by day, austere, close community life of a Carmelite is a martyrdom. All was done to please her Beloved, "Jesus, I would so love Him as He has never yet been loved before."

The cry of the dying Savior "I thirst!" resounded incessantly in her heart. The desire to quench His thirst for souls and win their love by a life of victimhood in imitation of her Master was always uppermost in her mind. She ever remained in spirit at the foot of the Cross to fill up that which is "lacking in the sufferings of Christ" (Col 1: 24). When Saint Thérèse said that she would remain at the foot of the Cross in order to receive and pour forth the divine dew of salvation upon souls, it was not just pious talk. She meant every word of it.

On one occasion the infirmarian put a hot water bottle to her feet and tincture of iodine on her chest. She was burning with fever and would have much preferred a glass of water. Her response: "My Jesus your child is thirsty! She is glad however to have this opportunity of resembling you more closely and thus of saving souls." Added to her physical suffering was the dark night of the soul and terrible temptations against the Faith. She told her sisters not to be alarmed if she died in total desolation, for did not Our Lord cry out from the Cross "My God, My God why have You abandoned me?" (Mk 15:35). Toward the end, she remarked to her sister that she didn't think it was possible to bear so much suffering, but added it was because of her great desire to save souls. On September 30, 1897, she died in a ecstasy of love gazing at her crucifix with the last words, "My God, I love You!" on her lips. She had predicted ". . .I think of all the good I shall do after my death. . .I will help priests, missionaries, the whole Church." Her promise of spending her heaven doing good upon earth was fulfilled in the innumerable graces and favors attributed to her intercession (see page 106). In reading St. Paul's description of the various vocations within the Mystical Body, the Church, she understood that the "Heart" was essential and embraced all vocations (missionary, teacher, martyr etc.), "Oh Jesus, my love, my vocation, I have found it at last. My vocation is Love!" Missionaries would surely lose their zeal were they not sustained by grace. This grace, ultimately won by the crucified Christ, is made effective in the work of every missionary through prayer and sacrifices.

Indeed, missionaries have found that by praying to her for help, their efforts in winning souls for Christ suddenly became more fruitful. We find St. Thérèse's missionary zeal and vocation summarized well in these words of St. Thérèse which are found on one side of the arch which spans the entrance to the nave of the basilica dedicated to her at Lisieux: "There is but one thing to be done here below: to love Jesus and to save souls."

Part IV

1. Pope John Paul II Declares — St. Thérèse, Doctor of the Church

2. St. Thérèse on the Priesthood

Rev. Thomas McKeon, S.S.S.

3. How St. Thérèse Found a Priest-Brother

Sr. Marie Immanuel, S.C.

4. Fraternal Charity of St. Thérèse

Jerry Kemper

Pope John Paul II Declares— St. Thérèse, Doctor of the Church

At the World Youth Day in August 1997 the Holy Father had made the announcement that he intended to enroll St. Thérèse of the Child Jesus a Doctor of the Church on Mission Sunday, October 19, 1997. The long awaited day (for there were many petitions, worldwide, seeking this honor for the saint) arrived. St. Peter's Square was bathed in a brilliant sunlight, with thousands of pilgrims as the Holy Father declared her "Doctor of the Universal Church."

The relics of the Saint were brought from Lisieux and carried in procession to be put in a place of honor before the altar of Sacrifice. When the Holy Father read the official proclamation, representatives from the six continents showered the reliquary and the crucifix with rose petals, as the choir sang in French verses from St. Thérèse's poem, **Jeter des fleurs.**

The Gospel was sung in Latin, the universal language of the Church, followed by the same text sung in Old Slavonic by a Russian deacon, recalling the fact that St. Thérèse was designated by the reigning pontiff, Pope Pius XI, as patroness of the Pontifical Russian College in Rome. At that time the Church in Russia was under severe persecution. After the Communion the famous passage from St. Thérèse's Story of a Soul, was read, "In the heart of the Church, my Mother, I will be love."

The Holy Father's Homily

"1. 'Nations shall come to your light' (Is 60:3). . ." *In the introduction of his homily on Mission Sunday the Holy Father speaks of the apostolic mission mandate to which Christ calls all men,* ". . . to accept in faith the saving Gospel. The Church is sent to all peoples, all lands and cultures: 'Go. . . and make disciples of all nations, baptizing them in the name of the Father and of the Son and of the Holy Spirit, teaching them to observe all that I have commanded you.' (Mt 28:19-20). . . .

"2. Thérèse Martin, a discalced Carmelite of Lisieux, ardently desired to be a missionary. She was one, to the point that she could be proclaimed patroness of the missions. Jesus himself showed her how she could live this vocation: by fully practicing the commandment of love, she would be immersed in the very heart of the Church's mission, supporting those who proclaim the Gospel with the mysterious power of prayer and communion. Thus she achieved what the Second Vatican Council emphasized in teaching that the Church is missionary by nature (cf. *Ad gentes,* n. 2). Not only those who choose the missionary life but all the baptized are in some way sent *ad gentes.*

"This is why I chose this missionary Sunday to proclaim St. Thérèse of the Child Jesus and the Holy Face *a doctor of the universal Church: a woman, a young person, a contemplative.*

"3. Everyone thus realizes that today something surprising is happening. St. Thérèse of Lisieux was unable to attend a university or engage in systematic study. She died young: nevertheless, from this day forward she will be honored as a doctor of the Church, an outstanding recognition which raises her in the esteem of the entire Christian community far beyond any academic title. Indeed, when the Magisterium proclaims someone a doctor of the Church, it intends to point out to all the faithful, particularly to those who perform in the Church the fundamental service of preaching or who undertake the delicate task of theological teaching and research, that the doctrine professed and proclaimed by a certain person can be a reference point, not only because it conforms to revealed truth, but also because it sheds new light on the mysteries of the faith, a deeper understanding of Christ's mystery. The Council reminded us that, with the help of the Holy Spirit, understanding of the 'depositum fidei' continually grows in the Church, and not only does the richly contemplative study to which theologians are called, not only does the Magisterium of pastors, endowed with the 'sure charism of truth,' contribute to this growth process, but also that *'profound understanding of spiritual things'* which is given *through experience,* with the wealth and diversity of gifts, to all those who let themselves be docilely led by God's Spirit (cf. *Dei Verbum,* n. 8). *Lumen gentium,* for its part, teaches that God himself 'speaks to us' (n. 50) in his saints. It is for this reason that the spiritual experience of the saints has a special value for deepening our knowledge of the divine mysteries, which remain ever greater than our thoughts, and not by chance does the Church choose only saints to be distinguished with the title of 'doctor.'

"4. Thérèse of the Child Jesus and the Holy Face is the youngest of all the 'doctors of the Church' but her ardent spiritual journey shows such

The relics of the Saint were brought to Rome for the solemn ceremony of St. Thérèse being enrolled as the 33rd Doctor of the Church. After the Pope read the proclamation, representatives from the six continents showered the reliquary and crucifix with rose petals. The Icon of St. Thérèse is from the Carmel in Lebanon showing the unity of the Church through the number of Doctors from both eastern and western Church.

Photos on page 68 & 69 from L'OSSERVATORE ROMANO

maturity, and the insights of faith expressed in her writings are so vast and profound that they deserve a place among the great spiritual masters.

"In the Apostolic Letter which I wrote for this occasion, I stressed several salient aspects of her doctrine. But how can we fail to recall here what can be considered its high point, starting with the account of the moving discovery of her special vocation in the Church? 'Charity', she wrote, 'gave me the key to my vocation. I understood that if the Church had a body composed of different members, the most necessary and most noble of all could not be lacking to it, and so I understood that the Church had a heart and that this heart was burning with love. I understood that it was love alone that made the Church's members act, that if love were ever extinguished, apostles would not proclaim the Gospel and martyrs would refuse to shed their blood. I understood that love includes all vocations. . . .Then in the excess of my delirious joy, I cried out: 'O Jesus, my Love . . . at last I have found my vocation; my vocation is Love!'" (*Ms B*, 3v). This is a wonderful passage which suffices itself to show that one can apply to St. Thérèse the Gospel passage we heard in the Liturgy of the Word: 'I thank you Father, Lord of heaven and earth, that you have hidden these things from the wise and understanding and revealed them to babes' (Mt 11:25).

"5. Thérèse of Lisieux did not only grasp and describe the profound truth of Love as the center and heart of the Church, but in her short life she lived it intensely. It is precisely this *convergence of doctrine and concrete experience,* of truth and life, of teaching and practice, which shines with particular brightness in this saint, and which makes her an attractive model especially for young people and for those who are seeking true meaning for their life.

"Before the emptiness of so many words, Thérèse offers another solution, the one Word of salvation which, understood and lived in silence, becomes a source of renewed life. She counters a rational culture, so often overcome by practical materialism, with the disarming simplicity of the "little way" which, by returning to the essentials, leads to the secret of all life: the divine Love that surrounds and penetrates every human venture. In a time like ours, so frequently marked by an ephemeral and hedonistic culture, this new doctor of the Church proves to be remarkably effective in enlightening the mind and heart of those who hunger and thirst for truth and love.

"6. St. Thérèse is presented as a doctor of the Church on the day we are celebrating World Mission Sunday. She had the ardent desire to dedicate herself to proclaiming the Gospel, and she would have liked to have crowned her witness with the supreme sacrifice of martyrdom (cf. *Ms B*,

3r). Moreover, her intense personal commitment supporting the apostolic work of Fr. Maurice Bellière and Fr. Adolphe Roulland, missionaries respectively in Africa and China, is well-known. In her zealous love for evangelization, Thérèse had one ideal, as she herself says: "What we ask of Him is to work for His glory, to love Him and to make Him loved" (*Letter* 220).

"The way she took to reach this ideal of life is not that of the great undertakings reserved for the few, but on the contrary, a way within everyone's reach, the 'Little Way,' a path of trust and total self-abandonment to the Lord's grace. It is not a prosaic way, as if it were less demanding. It is in fact a demanding reality, as the Gospel always is. But it is a way in which one is imbued with a sense of trusting abandonment to divine mercy, which makes even the most rigorous spiritual commitment light.

"Because of this way in which she receives everything as 'grace,' because she puts her relationship with Christ and her choice of love at the center of everything, because of the place she gives to the ardent impulses of the heart on her spiritual journey, Thérèse of Lisieux is a saint who remains young despite the passing years, and she is held up as an eminent model and guide on the path of Christians, as we approach the third millennium.

"7. Therefore the Church's joy is great on this day that crowns the expectations and prayers of so many who have understood, in requesting the title of doctor, this special gift of God and have supported its recognition and acceptance. We would all like to give thanks to the Lord together. . . .

"Yes, O Father, we bless you, together with Jesus (cf. Mt 11:25), because you have 'hidden your secrets from the wise and understanding' and have revealed them to this 'little one' whom today you hold up again for our attention and imitation.

"Thank you for the wisdom you gave her, making her an exceptional witness and teacher of life for the whole Church! Thank you, for the love you poured out upon her and which continues to illumine and warm hearts, spurring them to holiness. The desire Thérèse expressed to 'spend her heaven doing good on earth' (*Opere Complete*, p.1050), continues to be fulfilled in a marvelous way. Thank you, Father, for making her close to us today with a new title, to the praise and glory of your name for ever and ever. Amen!"

—L'OSSERVATORE ROMANO, Oct. 22, 1997

Sunday Angelus Talk on Thérèse, Doctor of the Church

In his Sunday "Angelus" talk after the Mass, the Holy Father stressed the important place Our Lady has in the spirituality of St. Thérèse:

". . .It could be said that *Thérèse* made her own the exceptional missionary vision of *Mary most holy*, who inspired the first apostolic community with her prayerful presence and perfect charity, so that the dynamism instilled by the Holy Spirit at Pentecost would carry the proclamation of the Gospel to the very ends of the earth.

"From early childhood *there was a deep bond between St. Thérèse of the Child Jesus and Mary.* She attributed her miraculous healing at the age of ten to the unforgettable experience of Mary's smile. . . .The spirit of filial abandonment to Our Lady, which marked little Thérèse's whole life, is offered to us today as an example to imitate. May St.Thérèse of the Child Jesus help us to love, follow and imitate the Blessed Virgin, Mother and Queen of all Saints." —L'OSSERVATORE ROMANO

Proclamation of St. Thérèse Doctor of the Church

Today, October 19, 1997, in St. Peter's square, filled with faithful from every part of the world and in the presence of a great many Cardinals, Archbishops and Bishops, during the solemn Eucharistic celebration, I proclaimed Thérèse of the Child Jesus and the Holy Face, a Doctor of the Universal Church in these words: **Fulfilling the wishes of many Brothers in the Episcopate and of a great number of the faithful throughout the world, after consulting the Congregation for the Causes of Saints and hearing the opinion of the Congregation for the Doctrine of Faith regarding her eminent doctrine, with certain knowledge and after lengthy reflection, with the fullness of Our apostolic authority We declare Saint Thérèse of the Child Jesus and the Holy Face, virgin, to be a Doctor of the Universal Church. In the name of the Father, and of the Son and of the Holy Spirit.**

His Holiness, Pope John Paul II

St. Thérèse and the Priesthood

By Rev. Thomas McKeon, S.S.S.

The following chapter first appeared in the Eucharistic magazine, THE LINK, which is a quarterly published in England. It is the voice of "The Eucharistic Union Pro Mundi Vita." .

FROM HER EARLIEST years St. Thérèse had a great intuitive understanding and veneration for the priesthood. It was from her father that she inherited her admiration and respect for the clergy. Speaking of him, her sister Céline said: "I have never seen anybody who had greater respect for the clergy. As a child, I imagined that all priests were gods, so accustomed were we to see them placed on a pedestal." To Thérèse priests were "as pure as crystal."

She became fully aware of the fact that they are vessels of clay, subject to the effects of original sin as all of us. In November 1887 at the age of 14 Thérèse and her sister Céline accompanied their father on a pilgrimage to Rome. There were 75 clerics in the group. Finding herself in their company in the train, in hotels and at table she saw that some seemed to forget the importance of prayer and effort in a life dedicated to God and the salvation of souls. Her reaction found expression in an intense desire to pray and offer sacrifices for the clergy. "The reason why I entered Carmel," she wrote in her autobiography, "I have declared before the Blessed Sacrament before making profession: 'I have come to save souls and especially to pray for priests.' Let us be apostles. Let us save souls especially the souls of priests." She developed the same thought on other occasions. "How sublime the vocation that aims to preserve the salt meant for souls! And this is the vocation of a Carmelite since the only purpose of our life of prayer and sacrifice is to be the apostles of the apostles while we pray for them as they go about preaching the Gospel by word but especially by example."

St. Thérèse prayed for the clergy that their ministry may yield abundant fruit. But she was also aware of the sad fact that some lived lives that shocked the faithful. "Alas!" she told her sister, "how many bad priests there are! They are not what they should be. Let us pray and suffer for them. . . .Céline, do you understand this cry that comes from the bottom of my heart?"

One of the priests whose defection saddened her most was the Carmelite friar, Hyacinth Loyson, a gifted preacher whose eloquence had drawn crowds to Notre Dame de Paris. In a letter dated July 30, 1870 he publicly declared that he had left the Church. Subsequently he married an American Protestant widow whom he had converted to Catholicism four years earlier. We trust that Thérèse's prayers were heard. He died in 1912 after kissing the crucifix while murmuring: "My gentle Jesus."

Were Thérèse living today would she join the ranks of those who clamor for a change in the tradition of the Church restricting ordination to the male sex? No doubt her fidelity to the doctrine and practice of the Church would not allow her to entertain the least doubt about the invalidity of orders conferred upon women. If she were here today she would unhesitatingly accept the declaration of Pope John Paul II:

"In order that all doubt may be removed regarding a matter of great importance, a matter which pertains to the Church's divine constitution, in virtue of my ministry of confirming the brethren (cf. Luke 22:33) I declare that the Church has no authority whatsoever to confer priestly ordination on women and that this judgment is to be definitively held by all the Church's faithful." (May 22, 1994)

Although she knew that the priesthood was out of the question for her and accepted the privation as the will of God, she still continued to long for ordination. She was very much like people filled with admiration for royalty and fancy themselves king or queen while realizing that they will never accede to the throne. Still in spite of her resignation to God's will the longing continued. "If only I were a priest," she wrote addressing Our Lord, "how lovingly, Jesus, would I hold you in my hands when my words had brought you down from heaven and how lovingly I would give you to the faithful! Yet while yearning for the priesthood I admire and envy the humility of Saint Francis of Assisi and I feel that my vocation is to imitate him by denying myself that sublime dignity."

The thought of priesthood never left her. Not long before dying she told her sister Céline: "See, God is calling me before one is old enough to be ordained this June. Well, so that I may not be disappointed, God permits this illness. I could not have made my way (to the Cathedral) and I would have died before exercising my ministry."

Instead of spending her time moaning over her inability to have her way, she found compensation in living to the full the priesthood all have in common. "Christ the Lord," says the Council, "the high priest chosen from among men (Cf. Heb 5:15) has made the new people's kingdom,

Fr. Adolphe Roulland, one of the two missionary priests whom St. Thérèse offered her prayers and sacrifices and occasionally corresponded. The co-patroness of the Missions, has adopted many priests making their mission fruitful.

priests to his God and Father (Rev 1:6). For by the regeneration and anointing of the Holy Spirit the baptized are consecrated as a spiritual dwelling and holy priesthood." (*Lumen Gentium* No. 10). She could not celebrate Mass but nothing prevented her from "offering herself as a living sacrifice consecrated to God and worthy of his acceptance" (Rom 12:1). She could not proclaim the word of God from the pulpit but her life as reflected through her autobiography taught us how to live the Gospel whatever our calling may be. And a hundred years after her death her autobiography continues to impact millions of people.

The words of the psalmist can most fittingly be applied to the diffusion of her message: "No word, no account of hers that does not make itself heard, her utterance fills every land, her message reaches the ends of the earth" (Ps 18, Knox Translation). A priest friend used to say: "I have been ordained almost fifty years and have dedicated my life to preaching, writing and parish work. And now I can say that the number of people

I have reached and influenced is infinitesimal compared with the multitude spiritually thriving on the wholesome doctrine they have found in St. Thérèse's works."

St. Thérèse's longing to be raised to the priesthood does not come as a surprise to those who realize that from her childhood she excelled in the spirit and the practice of magnanimity. She was endowed with a greatness of soul and heart that inclined her to do great things for God and the Church. Magnanimous souls are not expected to be involved in every possible noble enterprise. But they are always ready to translate their noble sentiments into action when the need arises. In longing for the priesthood St. Thérèse was consistent: she felt she was born for great things. First of all she wanted to be a saint. "I have the daring confidence," she said, "that one day I shall be a great saint. . .and mother of souls." But the love of Christ which inspired this noble dream could not remain inactive. "The love of Christ spurs us on."

"I long for other vocations," she wrote. "I want to be a warrior, a priest, an apostle, a doctor of the Church, a martyr. . . . I feel I would like to perform the most heroic deeds. I feel I have the courage of a Crusader. I should like to die on the battlefield in defense of the Church. . . . I should like to wander through the world, preaching Your name and raising Your Cross in pagan lands." Owing to the short span of 24 years allotted her and especially the cloistered life she had chosen, all these noble sentiments seemed to be mere wishful thinking. Not being able to realize all these vocations, including the priesthood, she felt that her special mission consisted in "being love in the Church." "I feel especially that I am about to enter upon my mission which consists in making God loved as I love Him and in sharing my Little Way with others. . . .Yes I want to spend my time in heaven doing good on earth. This is not impossible seeing that while enjoying the beatific vision the angels watch over us."

Thérèse's desire to be a saint has been realized and her holiness has been confirmed by the prodigies wrought through her intercession and officially recognized by the Church. The teaching that permeated her life and guided her continues to influence many of the faithful in different parts of the world and led to her being officially recognized as a Doctor of the Church. Her interest in the missions expressed by the power of her intercession for the fruitful ministry of countless missionaries has prompted the Church to declare her Patron of the Missions alongside St. Francis Xavier. She has helped and inspired many priests, whom she seems to have adopted, exercise their priesthood in the spirit and zeal that would have marked her ministry.

Bl. Théophane Vénard the young martyred missionary, for whom St. Thérèse had a special devotion. She wrote about him, "Oh I would very much like to have a picture of Théophane Vénard; he is a kindred soul. St. Aloysius Gonzaga was serious, even in recreation, but Théophane Vénard was always happy." Thérèse was drawn to him after reading a biography of his life and martyrdom. Similar to herself, besides a happy temperament, he had great affection for family members.

Many good people suffer today because priests they know and hold in high esteem do not live up to their expectations. At times they learn that a friend or relative has decided to "resign from the priesthood" as if he were a lawyer who has chosen to abandon his profession to become involved with politics. The grief one experiences is more intense when the change is compounded by an attempted marriage. Instead of yielding to frustration as if nothing could be done let them look to Saint Thérèse who became a Carmelite to pray and offer sacrifices for priests. She adopted missionaries for whom she prayed in a special way. She offered sacrifices so that Fr. Loyson would recover the faith he had lost. Like our Blessed Mother, "she was taken to heaven so that she might plead for us with greater confidence" (Cf. Prayer over the Gifts, Pre-Vat. Rite, Vigil of Assumption). It is inconceivable then that she should turn a deaf ear to the supplications of those who seek to enlist her interest in the priests who are remiss in their duties or have strayed from the fold.

Most of the quotations are taken from Thérèse et L'Eucharistie Annales de Ste Thérèse, April 1981. Permission granted by Rector of Pilerinage Sainte Thérèse de Lisieux.

How St. Thérèse Found a Priest-Brother

Sr. Marie Immanuel, S.C.

"She has received a mission to teach priests a greater love of Jesus Christ." *—Pope Benedict XV*

Saint Thérèse of Lisieux herself frequently spoke of her intense desire to offer her life that priests might be holy, praying not only for her two adopted missionary "brothers," but for all priests. That her concern for priestly souls continues now, though Thérèse has long since left Carmel for heaven, is proven by the unusual story of Fr. Vernon Johnson who, when the Little Flower first entered his life, was a priest in the Anglican Church and a friar in an Anglo-Catholic religious order.

To appreciate what wonders Thérèse worked for Friar Vernon in bringing him to Rome, one must understand how firmly he was entrenched in Anglo-Catholicism. His sister's account of his life before he encountered Thérèse makes it clear how impossible it would have seemed to Father Vernon himself or to those who knew him best that he would ever be touched by "Roman Fever."

He had hardly ever been inside a Catholic church; he knew no Catholic priests, he experienced no uneasiness about his attraction to things Roman, considering it only as a treasured inheritance from the Oxford Movement. But Miss Johnson's account also details the popular young friar's love for Christ and for his poorest ones, and Vernon's gifts as preacher and spiritual director.

Vernon Johnson was born into a well-to-do English family in 1886, and entered an Episcopalian seminary from college to study for the priesthood. Ordained in 1910, his first assignment was curate in the desolate slums of Brighton, a coastal town in England. Three arduous years there, however, left him unsatisfied; things were still "too easy," and he longed for the stricter discipline of a religious order. Consequently, in the spring of 1914, he entered the Anglo-Catholic Society of Divine Compassion, and after a brief formation period, Father Vernon, wearing a Franciscan habit, set off on his first assignment as a religious. It was an assignment which gives some measure of his priestly character even then: With another friar and two nurses, he was to open and direct a home for English lepers. Two years later, Saint Giles was a well-established hospice where England's few lepers were welcomed with love to spend their remaining days in dignity and peace.

From Saint Giles, Father Vernon was sent to London's East End, "a dark and frightening place," wrote Miss Johnson, "where poverty and misery dwelt and men fought for mere existence." Father Vernon had barely settled there when the Spanish flu, epidemic throughout Europe, was carried to England and raged unconfined through the slums. The Brothers from the East End House of Divine Compassion, acting as undertakers for the poor, often buried fifty people a day and then returned to the poor dwellings to pray with the dying and comfort the bereaved.

To add to the distress of those months, devastating raids by enemy aircraft often brought incalculable destruction to the thickly-populated neighborhood, where the flimsy houses offered no protection from fire or bombs. Since there were no established places of refuge from air attacks in the East End, Father Vernon and the other Brothers used to go from house to house, to be with their people during those awful hours. After the final war raid in May, 1918, they returned to their own little House of Compassion to find that it had been completely demolished; only the crucifix was left, still hanging on a shattered door.

After the war, Father Vernon served in different houses of his society, becoming much sought after both as a preacher and as a spiritual director. Canon Gordon Albion, in a biographical sketch, noted that, "his good looks were enhanced by his Franciscan habit and still more by his innate sense of style and flair in the pulpit, bringing him crowds of young socialites and debutantes to hear him preach." Thérèse must have realized that it was high time she intervened. And so it happened that when Father Vernon went to a convent to make a retreat late in 1924, the first rose was sent tumbling down to him: The Anglican sister in charge of the house offered him *The Story of a Soul* for his spiritual reading.

Father Vernon demurred. "No, thanks," he said, handing it back. "It's French—and it's Roman Catholic." "Don't be prejudiced," the sister admonished. "Take it and read it; you'll like it."

Humbly, Father Vernon took the autobiography to his room. The first two chapters did not reassure him; in fact, he found them distressingly cloying, just as he had expected. His first impression, he told a friend later, was, "What an appalling pious little prig!" But he read on and then—then Thérèse began to emerge, and Father Vernon read until early morning, read until he had turned the last page. The simple story moved him as no other book ever had. Five years later, trying to explain to stunned friends why he was submitting to Rome, he wrote of that first encounter with Thérèse:

Here was someone who had loved Our Lord to a degree beyond anything I had ever seen before: a love as strong as that of the martyrs of old, and yet with the delicacy and tenderness of a little child, so delicate and tender that one almost fails to realize the furnace in which that love was wondrously refined. Above all else, it was the Saint's gospel of suffering as being the most blessed gift, by which alone we could be really united to our Blessed Lord in unfettered love, and her interpretation of pain and suffering as something which can be offered in union with our Blessed Lord's cross for the sake of the Church and for the salvation of souls—it was all this which, coming into my life when things were exceedingly difficult, lit up and made real to me certain spiritual truths towards which I was dimly groping; truths which I had been discouraged from holding as being morbid and so forth, and which I now found were the very foundations of the saintly life. . . . For over six months the study of this book pulled me through one of the most difficult passages of my life.

"I find here my own thoughts, word for word, my own spiritual experiences," he confided to his beloved sister while discussing the book with her. "From that moment," she remembered, "he had no peace." Five crucifying years were to pass before he could take the irrevocable step which knowing Thérèse had made mandatory for him. He went to Lisieux with other pilgrims. "My first impression," he wrote, "was one

Vernon Johnson in the Franciscan habit of an Anglo-Catholic religious. Johnson (right) with his friend Ronnie Knox who later also joined the Catholic Church and became a Monsignor. He too had a great love of St. Thérèse and translated her biography into English.

of great repulsion; it was all so foreign, sentimental and artificial." But the sense of strangeness, the disappointment, left him in the Carmelites' Hall of Relics. There, he was deeply moved to see so many things Thérèse had used during her brief religious life.

His visit to Les Buissonnets, Thérèse's childhood home, was also a touching experience. He did not need a guide as he moved from room to room; the autobiography had made everything familiar. Like other tourists, he looked reverently at the mementos, all carefully shielded behind glass partitions, her copybook, her rosary, her own small desk, her skipping rope and top. The contrast between the toys and the scourge he had seen at the convent seemed to Father Vernon to epitomize the story of Thérèse's life, "a perfect parable of the power of Divine Grace." He was charmed by the pretty walled garden, too, recalling how Thérèse as a little girl had spent happy hours there, playing or "thinking." He did not dream that the next day would find him a prisoner there, yet that is what happened. For his little saint, in her own characteristic way, had set out to secure a special favor for her client, now that he was actually in Lisieux: a private meeting with the prioress, Mother Agnes of Jesus, Thérèse's beloved "little mother."

Consequently, when Father Vernon returned to the garden late that afternoon to pray, the sister-guardian, not realizing that there were still guests on the premises, locked the garden gate and all the doors, pocketed the keys, and went off. To the staid Father Vernon's chagrin, he and a young Belgian priest who had joined him in the garden and with whom he had been lost in conversation, had to seek a ladder, scale the wall, and then, by making a most unseemly racket, try to attract the attention of neighbors who could assist them down from their high perches.

Because of the misadventure, he was late for dinner at the hotel. Because he was late, he was seated with a newcomer. Because the newcomer insisted that they visit the cemetery where Thérèse's mother is buried, Father Vernon grudgingly accompanied him. Because he was in the cemetery just at that time, he encountered a woman tending a grave, who introduced herself as a classmate of the saint. Because the lady took an interest in the Protestant clergyman from England, she offered to try to arrange for him to speak with Mother Agnes. And because the Little Flower was undoubtedly pushing the whole affair, Mother Agnes agreed, although the nuns had not been granting interviews that week, due to canonization business!

The next morning found Father Vernon kneeling at the white-curtained grille in the little parlor where Thérèse as a child had knelt in floods of tears, talking to this same loved sister. Father Vernon opened his heart

Monsignor Vernon Johnson in 1963. In the three happy decades as a Catholic priest he dedicated his life to spreading the Little Way through carrying on her apostolate to priests, organizing the Association of the Priests of St. Thérèse, editing *Sicut Parvuli*, a quarterly review for the associates, giving retreats and days of recollection steeped in Thérèsian theology geared to priestly needs.

to her. "You must react," she told him. But he dismissed the advice without a scruple, sure that the holy Roman Catholic nun did not realize that he already enjoyed and treasured, as an Anglo-Catholic, everything that Rome could offer him: the Mass, the Sacraments, Our Lady, even religious life, which he had been living for years in various houses of Divine Compassion as a Franciscan friar. That brief visit was the spiritual highlight of his entire pilgrimage, and he was sure he owed it to Thérèse.

"I was conscious," he wrote years later, "that my visit was being guided in a mysterious way. At first, it seemed coincidence...but as time went on, I knew it was more than mere coincidence which led me, a stranger and all unknown, to kneel in the Carmel parlor and receive the blessing of Mother Agnes, the saint's own sister; I must believe it was the prayers of the little saint herself."

Though he was back in London in less than a week, he realized that he had been through a spiritual experience unlike anything he had ever known before. What Father Vernon encountered firsthand, he knew, was a love of God such as he had never met before. "The deity of Christ," he said, "was flashed before my soul at Lisieux with blinding splendor. My soul drank deep there at the pure stream of the undiluted truth of the Godhead of my Lord. . . . I had been where the unseen was very, very near, and where the veil was very, very thin."

The Catholic Church as such, however, did not attract him even then. His experience gave him no desire to become a Catholic and no thought that he would ever be one. He went home resolving instead, to try to make the devotion to Christ in the Blessed Sacrament, as he had seen it at Lisieux and knew it in Thérèse's life, "the very life and breath of the Church of England."

And with that resolution, he settled down again to work for souls as an Anglican religious.

"I Shall Be a Catholic"

A year later Father Johnson returned to Lisieux. His second visit made him aware that he could no longer evade the challenges he met there. WAS the Church which had produced a Saint Thérèse of the Child Jesus, he asked himself a thousand times over, WAS that the TRUE Church? Here apparently, was real sanctity: how was that possible in the context of the modern world? Besides such sanctity must have been rooted in the absolutism of faith, which in turn would depend on the living authority of the Church. Could he find that authority in the Church of England? As he said goodby after this second visit, he told the nuns soberly, "When I come back, I shall be a Catholic." But he admitted later that he simply couldn't even contemplate ever taking such a step.

After his death his sister explained just what "going over to Rome" had cost him. "It meant a clean break," she wrote. "Church, career, friends,

Monsignor Johnson (seated third from the left) with his first Priest's Pilgrimage to Lisieux in 1937.

all had to be sacrificed. Above all, the thought of his flock troubled him, the thousands of souls who followed him . . . .He had to leave them all, and none of them would understand the step he was taking. The many people who afterwards condemned him for his selfishness had no idea of the *via dolorosa* of those years."

For a sensitive nature like Father Vernon's, the pain resulting merely from the thought of hurting those who loved him was almost unbearable. He confided to the Carmelites at Lisieux that he often woke at night crying to God, "You cannot ask this of me: I cannot do it!" But an even more sacred obligation was holding him back: the role he felt that he perhaps should play in the rapidly increasing degree of Catholic life in the Church of England, as he saw it, for example, in the extraordinary increase in English contemplatives.

A Seminarian Again at Age 43

Characteristically, while he prayed and deliberated and suffered, Thérèse continued her delicate little attentions. (She definitely would NOT take no for an answer!) Finally, five years after he had first opened her autobiography, and three years after his second trip to Lisieux had overwhelmed him with doubts he could not handle, Vernon Johnson was received into the Catholic Church. Then, leaving everything he had known and loved, he went to Rome to begin at 43 his preparation for the Catholic priesthood.

During his long course of studies at the Beda, Saint Thérèse's seminarian delved deeper into the mysteries of her "Little Way," struggling to incorporate it into every area of his life, to build his prayer on it, to share it with others. From the start, he had seen in it what many of Thérèse's admirers never grasp: that Thérèse's "way" is the way of the cross, utilizing suffering for holiness.

Now, he discovered that it was primarily a Gospel message, too, based on Our Lord's own words, "Unless you become as little children, you shall not enter the Kingdom of Heaven."

Important also was the papal approval: the new convert was doggedly loyal to the Holy See. And it was a Pauline way; he rejoiced in that. Thérèse often quoted Saint Paul—and Vernon quoted both of them, becoming more and more aware of just what Thérèse had to say to him, to priests, to all the faithful.

In June, 1933, at the age of 49, Vernon Johnson went home to England to be ordained a Catholic priest, and within a fortnight, he was in Lisieux, to say Mass for the nuns who had done so much to pray him to his goal. Thérèse intervened again, this time with a favor he never dreamed of: The Bishop of Lisieux, whom he met unexpectedly, gave him permission to visit inside the cloister, a privilege so rare as to be unheard of. As the cloister door was unbolted for him, he dropped to his knees to kiss the sill; Thérèse had entered through that doorway the day she came to Carmel. That blessed afternoon he was permitted to pray to his heart's content in her tiny cell, in the chapter room where she had made her vows, and in the choir where she had spent so many hours every day. Thérèse's culminating ordination gift came the next morning: He was invited to offer his Mass in the bare little infirmary room where she had suffered and died, the chalice he used being the one Thérèse had so often handled when she was sacristan, the one she holds in the photograph one so often sees of her in the sacristy. "In that hour," wrote his sister, "he regained his peace."

What Father Johnson did for and with Thérèse in his three happy decades in the Catholic priesthood makes another story, for he dedicated his life to spreading her Little Way, especially carrying on for her apostolate to priests, organizing the Association of the priests of Saint Thérèse, editing *Sicut Parvuli*, a quarterly review for the associates, and spending himself in giving retreats and days of recollection steeped in the Thérèsian theology he realized was so geared to priestly needs.

The Rosary, His Source of Comfort

Another story might center around his lifelong love of Our Lady, which burgeoned under Thérèse's tutelage until, in the weakness of old age, he had his rosary always in his hands, finding in it his constant source of comfort and his final quiet effort to walk Thérèse's Little Way to God. The sister-nurse who was with him on night duty in his illness recalled that, toward the end, visitors tired him very quickly, but that he never tired of having someone pray the rosary with him and would always thank them for their kindness.

Mindful to the last of Thérèse's desire to bring priests closer to Christ, he said wistfully to his nurse just before he died, "Sister, I don't feel that I've done as much as I should have done for priests." She reassured him and he smiled and said, "Thank you, Sister! Now I am very happy." These were his last words. He died in 1969 at the age of eighty. Thérèse's protégé had used well the roses she had showered down on him for so many years!

*Reprinted with Permission from September 1978, **Immaculata***

Fraternal Charity of St. Thérèse

Jerry Kemper

In her autobiography, Thérèse points out that charity gave her the key to her vocation: "I understood that since the Church is a body composed of different members,. . . therefore, the Church has a heart—and a heart on fire with love. I saw, too, . . . that should love ever fail, apostles would no longer preach the Gospel and martyrs would refuse to shed their blood. Finally, I realized that love includes every vocation, that love is all things, that love is eternal, . . . I cried out, Jesus, my Love, my vocation is found at last, my vocation is love!" Prayer and sacrifice ever motivated by love is the fulcrum as Thérèse points out that we can "lift the world." Thérèse certainly offered every opportunity she found to please Jesus and to win souls, all expressions of an uncompromising love of God.

But the most obvious opportunities to offer "little sacrifices" to the Lord escapes most of us. It all depends upon a supernatural outlook as to how we view our neighbors and how we put into practice the words of St. John, "How can we say we love God if we do not show it by our love for our neighbor?" It is precisely here more than anywhere else that the authenticity of the Little Way is made visible in the life and virtues practiced by St. Thérèse. An example: In the last few months of her life when she was dying a slow agonizing death, she was placed outside of the infirmary for a few hours to enjoy a little sunshine. As she lay there putting the finishing touches on the manuscript of her life under obedience of two superiors, sisters passing by on their way to the field with hoes and sickles in hand, would stop to and from and make small talk with her to "cheer her up." One of her sisters asked her if this wasn't a distraction and an unwanted interruption in her writing. She replied: "How can I write about charity if I do not show charity to my well intentioned fellow sisters."

In her *Story of a Soul* we read how she meditated and took to heart the passage of Our Lord in Scripture, "Love one another as I have loved you." She readily admitted "How imperfect was the love I bore my sisters in religion; I did not love them as Our Lord does. Now, I know that true charity consists in bearing all my neighbor's defects, in not being surprised at mistakes, but in being edified at the smallest virtues. I hasten to look for a sister's virtues and good motives. I call to mind that though I may have seen her fall once, she may have gained many victories over herself which in her humility she conceals, and also that what appears to be a fault may very well, owing to the good intention that prompted it, be an act of virtue." How perfectly this fulfills the admonition of Christ "Judge not and you will not be judged." And again, in her own words, "What gives us greater peace and joy than to think well of our neighbor?" All this is above and beyond ordinary human charity and capability. So she had resort to Him who *is* Charity.

"Jesus, You know that I shall never love my sisters as You have loved them, unless You love them Yourself within me, my dearest Master. It is because You desire to grant me this grace, that You have given a new Commandment, and dearly do I cherish it, since it proves to me that it is Your Will to love in me all those You have bid me to love.'

In reading her *Story of a Soul*, one is impressed throughout by the extraordinary delicacy and thoughtfulness she showed her fellow religious. At times she even resorted to tough love. She was not easy or over indulgent to the novices under her direction (See chapter on page 49). When only eighteen years old she noticed a religious some years older than she, who found every excuse she could to visit Mother Prioress. An inordinate attachment was developing that would eventually be detrimental to the future of this sister. There is a provision in the Carmelite Constitutions that provided conversations between sisters to foster virtue. So she did not hesitate to warn the sister: "Since we meet regularly to help each other develop virtues, sister, you know, I think you go to see Mother Prioress too often." Sister Thérèse was taking a chance as the sister could have gone directly to the Prioress to repeat the remark. Knowing that her companion in the novitiate would ever speak the truth that sister in question accepted the charitable admonition and a vocation was possibly saved, at least pointed in the right direction.

Another sister who was a workaholic, at the end of the day was totally exhausted and could have easily succumbed to temptations. Since Sister Thérèse could not cheer her up with a kind word during the evening grand silence, she stood near her cell to give the sister a kindly smile as she passed by. After St. Thérèse's death that sister remarked, "O, that smile of Sister Thérèse! It seemed to me as if all my troubles vanished!" Another elderly nun who had an "allergy" to the scent of roses noticed a bouquet of artificial roses Thérèse had arranged. Before the nun could react, Thérèse took one of the roses and turning to her said: "You see, dear Sister, how well they imitate nature these days." The nun immediately "felt better."

One sister whom no one could please was understandably avoided by her fellow religious. Thérèse noticed that she needed help at times but there was not one to assist her. So she went to the Mother Prioress and asked if she could sit near her and assist her. Mother, all too willingly, acceded to her request. She assisted this nun in her work according to her every little whim and fancy. Each time Thérèse felt annoyance she would "offer it up" and give the sister a sweet smile. After Thérèse's death, one day at community recreation the sisters were reminiscing about how she had shown sisterly love to each. This sister exclaimed: "Oh, yes. Sister Thérèse was so kind, so good, so loving. As for me, I have no regrets in her regard, because whenever she worked with me I always seemed to make her so happy." What strength of will and charity this implies of St. Thérèse.

Everyone is sensitive to others "borrowing" a clever, or even wise statement we may have made, or even a piece of news, claiming it as their own. In her deep charity and spiritual poverty, claiming absolutely nothing as her own, St. Thérèse was pleased to be the hidden and anonymous source. During her life, when she was missing from common recreation, the sisters would say: "We won't have much fun today, because Sister Thérèse isn't here." Contrary to some misrepresentations of the saints as dour, always serious kill joys, Sister Thérèse was the "life of the party." She entertained the community with her witty remarks and even cleverly mimicked the preachers they had heard. As mentioned in another chapter, she was a great story teller.

Even in consecrated religious life, it is too easy not to rise above natural friendships that would be detrimental to spiritual progress and community living. We all have our friends and favorites to be invited into our inner selves and confidences, as was already mentioned in this chapter. In the past this was accurately called what it actually is, "particular friendships," and friendship that would exclude other members of the community.

St. Thérèse rose above this in a heroic way, and shows us how we too can do the same. She too had the temptation to single out other sisters, her own blood sisters in particular, for affection and conversation, which is, of course, discouraged in religious life. When her sister Pauline (Mother Agnes of Jesus in religious life) became Mother Prioress, the temptation to find excuses and reasons to visit with her were so strong that she had to grab the banister to remind herself of the motivations that would be contrary to the spirit of the rule. She did not in any way show favoritism to her blood sisters, to such an extent that they complained to her that she no longer seemed to love them.

On the other hand, how she was able to overcame a natural antipathy was related in her autobiography. In her own words: "A holy nun of our community annoyed me in all she did. I did not want to yield to my natural antipathy, for I remembered that charity ought to betray itself in deeds and not to exist merely in feelings. So I set myself to do for this sister all I should do for the one I loved most. . . . One day she said to me, with beaming face: 'My dear Sister Thérèse, tell me what attraction you find in me. Whenever we meet you greet me with such a sweet smile.' Ah, what attracts me was Jesus hidden in the depths of her soul." Only after St. Thérèse's death and her autobiography was read to the community, did this sister recognize that she was the one referred to by our saint.

To rise to such heights of fraternal charity requires a life made up of hidden sacrifices based on humility, confidence in the Father's love and one's response to that love. In the Gospel we read: "Love your enemies (Read: those with whom we do not get along); do good to them that hate you; pray for them that persecute you and calumniate you; that you may be the children of your Father that is in heaven. . . . Be you perfect, as your heavenly Father is perfect" (Mt 5:44-48).

And so St. Thérèse again simplifies for us what it takes to become a saint. It is exactly in this fidelity of little daily sacrifices to show our love for God and to please Jesus through our love of neighbor.

The Carmelite Community in Lisieux during the time that St. Thérèse was a member (See if the reader can find Thérèse).

Part V

Is This Book for the
Spiritual Elite?

By Fr. Pacificus Kennedy, OFM

One winter evening in 1895, two-and-a-half years before she died, Thérèse was laughing with two of her sisters over childhood memories. That gave Marie, her oldest sister and her godmother (Sr. Marie of the Sacred Heart) an idea. She said to Pauline, the second oldest Martin girl, who was prioress at the time, "Ah, Mother Agnes, how nice it will be if you get Thérèse to write these memories for us." Pauline smiled and said to her baby sister, "I command you to write your childhood memories."

Thérèse thought this a joke, "What could I write that you don't know already?" When she perceived Pauline had given a gentle command, she prepared to comply. Her sister Léonie, nine and a half years older and still living in Lisieux after their father's death, brought her a black-covered copybook. Thérèse asked the Blessed Virgin to guide her pen. Day by day, after working and praying from early morn, she spent her only free time, about a half hour after Compline, writing in her cell by the light of a tiny oil lamp. She completed this family souvenir, which became the first eight chapters of her autobiography, for the feast day of Mother Agnes, January 21, 1896. She casually handed it to her in chapel with a smile and a bow.

Then Marie asked her to tell about the secrets Jesus had made known to her. So between September 3rd and 16th, 1896, Thérèse wrote the ten closely crammed pages (not in the copybook) of her letter to Marie. The many corrections indicate haste and fatigue. This became the last chapter (XIII), entitled *A Canticle of Love,* of the autobiography.

By the summer of 1897 everyone knew that Thérèse's life was tapering off. In 1896, unknown to the community, she had suffered a lung hemorrhage on Holy Thursday night in her cell, and had hoped to die on Good Friday. She reported it to the prioress, but seemed to cover up her deteriorating health to the community. But when it was known how critical her health was and uncertain how much longer she had to live, Pauline showed the copybook to the prioress, Mother Gonzague. She asked her to command Thérèse to write something "a little more serious" about her life as a nun, so there would be something to say in her obituary (the letter sent to other Carmels at the death of each nun).

Sitting in a wheelchair under the chestnut trees in the garden, Thérèse resumed writing in the copybook on June 3, 1897. She was constantly interrupted by goodhearted nuns who thought it was just as easy to lay down a pen as a rake. Pauline got impatient about this, but not Thérèse. "I'm supposed to be writing about brotherly love," she said. "This is a chance to show I believe in it." She retained her equanimity even though she was being subjected at the time to a horrible remedy for tuberculosis by the local doctor, cauterizing. This treatment called *pointes de feu* (points of fire) consisted of heating needles and plunging them into the flesh. Her sister Celine (Sr. Geneviève of the Holy Face) counted 500 *pointes de feu* on Thérèse's back. Nevertheless, early in July she completed the third part of her script, addressed to Mother Gonzague. It became Chapters IX to XII of the autobiography. When the copybook was filled she finished by writing on the back of a calendar. Each of the three sections ends with the same word: Love.

But the nuns did not realize they had a saint on their hands. Sister Vincent de Paul said: "She has never done anything worth mentioning. What will they say in the obituary?" Other nuns said worse. Pauline wanted Thésèse to speak for herself. The Prioress agreed to send an edition of the document to other Carmels only and on two conditions: first, it must be corrected, polished and approved by Dom Godfrey Madelaine, a friend of the Carmel who knew Thérèse; second, it must be entirely recast to make it appear that all three parts had been addressed to Mother Gonzague. Pauline did not fear to agree because of the generous commission Thérèse had given her. Dom Godfrey wielded his blue pencil freely, divided the manuscript into chapters, and actually gave it a good title: *Story of a Soul.* The prioress supervised the entire project. Several decades later it was revealed, to the horror of some historians and critics, that at least 7,000 changes of various kinds had been made. What must be kept uppermost in mind, however, is that this fervent, artless, truncated autobiography — this non-book by a non-writer — became the vehicle which made known the nun whom Pius X, long before her canonization, called "the greatest saint of modern times." When the printer delivered 2,000 copies to the Carmel, September 1898, a nun exclaimed, "What will we ever do with all these?"

Replies from other Carmels were not entirely sympathetic. "This life was infantile and not at all in harmony with the austerity of Carmel."

"Age and experience would have changed her opinions about spiritual matters." "The thought that this manuscript is now free for anyone to read distresses me beyond words," said an Irish prioress, "If this justifies Thérèse Martin in being canonized, then all my nuns will qualify for it when their turn comes." Such purblind reactions show the need of the work theologians have been doing with the saint's writings.

Other Carmels, on the other hand, began loaning out the pamphlet (such it was) to relatives and benefactors. The original printing was quickly exhausted. Translations began to appear. Missionaries in the boondocks rendered their favorite passages in native dialects. When people craved to know more about Thérèse, Pauline was able to respond but did not tell everything all at once. During Thérèse's last eighteen months, Pauline had written on scraps of paper everything she heard her say. Eventually she filled five green-covered copybooks for the Process of the Cause. Then she filled one yellow-covered copybook with her sister's last conversation. Additional information came from a memoir written by one of the five novices Thérèse companioned during her last four years.

Pius XI could not have known what a cross he was laying on Pauline when he made her prioress for life in 1923. Fifty-four of her sixty-nine years in Carmel were devoted to the spread of her sister's teachings. She was harried with all kinds of conflicting advice. But she actually took on the Congregation of Rites and won a victory. The 9th Lesson for Matins of St. Thérèse's feast reads ". . . *inflamed with the desire of suffering,* she offered herself, two years before her death, as a victim to the merciful love of God." Pauline did not rest till she persuaded that authority to change that to ". . . *on fire with divine love, etc.*," which is a faithful expression of Theresian thought. Thérèse was in love with God, not in love with suffering for its own sake. "The soul offering herself to love is not asking for suffering," Celine learned from Thérèse. "But in yielding herself up entirely to the demands of love she is accepting in advance all that Divine Providence will be pleased to send her by way of joys, labors, trials. At the same time she counts on Infinite Mercy to enable her to sanctify her crosses by an enduring spirit of joy."

Before she died in 1951, Pauline said to Celine, her last remaining sister, "After my death I order you to publish the original texts in my name." Pauline was severely criticized when the facsimile edition of the original texts was published (French only, of course) in 1956. Some purists objected that in the original Zelie Guerin Martin called her daughter Thérèse a *nervous child,* whereas in her edition Pauline called her *an exuberant child.* Both were right. Celine cleared up many difficulties when, in November 1957, two years before she died, she reread and ap-

The interior of the Basilica of St. Thérèse in Lisieux

proved all the notes she had written about Thérèse over the years. Her *Memoir of My Sister St. Thérèse* is an invaluable complement to the autobiography.

Is this Spiritual Childhood teaching, as contained in the spiritual classic *Story of a Soul,* for the elite and innocent? No! It is for the guilty, the hardened, the sophisticated, the despairing:

"I am certain that even if I had every imaginable crime," says the Saint, "I should lose nothing of my confidence. Rather would I hasten with a heart broken with sorrow to throw myself into the arms of Jesus. He cherished the prodigal son."

In the opinion of Dominican Father H. Petitot, "It will be some centuries before the prodigious and many-sided influence of St. Thérèse can be exactly appreciated. Then it will be recognized that she has been the principal and providential promoter of a new epoch."

— *Friar Magazine*

A Book Never Intended to Be a Book

If St. Thérèse's "Little Way of Spiritual Childhood" is known throughout the world, it is due in no small measure to the worldwide circulation of her autobiography, *Story of a Soul*. John Beevers, in the introduction to his translation of St. Thérèse's autobiography, claims with good reason, that this book is "the great best seller of this century."

"When we pick up *Story of a Soul,* we are handling something akin to a miracle. We have a book which was never written as a book. It was scribbled very quickly and produced in three parts, each addressed to a different person. Much of it was written when its author knew she was dying and was suffering all the pain and distress of a fatal illness. Now, it is the most widely read book of spirituality in the world and is acclaimed by popes for the sureness of its teaching. . . As St. Thérèse sat in her cell and wrote, her companion was the Holy Spirit. Her book was divinely inspired, not, it must be understood, as Holy Scripture was inspired, but inspired as perhaps no other book has been." Though not by an accomplished writer, of its style, which is more the product of that particular time in France, Beevers points out: "There burns a fierce, exultant flame of holy passion, and it is this passion which grips the reader — sometimes at once, but nearly always after a second or third reading."

This fire has inflamed many famous personages. One of these was the famous Chinese scholar, Doctor John C. H. Wu. He wrote after his conversion to the Catholic faith: "Dante was my guide to the threshold of the Church, but the ones who made me cross it were the most holy Virgin and her little daughter, St. Thérèse of Lisieux." Dr. Wu, a former Methodist, read *Story of a Soul* and found that it expressed perfectly the more profound convictions he had about Christianity. He exclaimed: "If this saint represents Catholicism, I do not see any reason why I should not be a Catholic."

He goes on to say, "For I found in it a living synthesis of joy and suffering, duty and love, strength and tenderness, grace and nature, wisdom and folly, wealth and poverty, community and individualism. The Saint seemed to combine within herself the compassion of Buddha, the virtues of Confucius and the philosophical detachment of Lao Tze. Here is a young nun who died at 24 and still managed to attain such perfection! What was her secret? Could she have achieved such plenitude if she had not been a part of the Mystical Body of Christ?"

Another great scholar and Catholic writer, Jean Guitton, writes: "The strange thing about Thérèse, young and uneducated as she is, is the authority with which she teaches her way. It is this radical authority which, in spite of all her inexperience, has reminded some people of Joan of Arc. She is a child without childhood and outside childhood."

A most unusual reader of the Autobiography and follower of her "Little Way" was a criminal who was eventually guillotined. Twenty-seven-year-old Jacques Fesch through his inspiring spiritual diaries, written after his conversion, is considered another St. Dismas and may be beatified some day. He writes: "Like little Saint Thérèse of the Child Jesus, I would like to renew with every beat of my heart, the offering of myself as a holocaust victim to God's merciful love. . . . I wait in darkness and in peace. . . . I am waiting for love! In five hours, I will be with Jesus!"

One of the greatest "conquests" of St. Thérèse and her autobiography was the late Msgr. Vernon Johnson, who caused a great stir in the Church of England when he became a Catholic and then later was ordained a Catholic priest. (See article on page 78). He wrote possibly the most popular book available on her spirituality, titled, "Spiritual Childhood." He organized priest pilgrimages to Lisieux, for he was well aware of the fact that this saintly Carmelite is perhaps the priests' best friend, after Our Lord and Our Lady. He published the magazine "Sicut Parvuli," a quarterly review of the Association of Priests of St. Thérèse of the Child Jesus. (Several chapters in our book were taken from this publication.) He was its editor and publisher for twenty years until his death in 1969.

An amusing conversion story is that of the American reporter, Eddie Doherty. While on the staff of the old "Liberty" magazine, he had to cover a story about the famous radio priest of the thirties, Fr. Charles Coughlin. Though Eddie was a fallen away Catholic, he figured he had to get some background material on the patron saint of Fr. Coughlin's church. At first, he confused St. Rita with the "Little Flower." It took a good deal of convincing on the part of the sales woman at the book store to get him to accept the Autobiography of St. Thérèse. "No book has ever stirred me as did that simple, beautiful story, written by a girl in her 20s, a nun shivering in her cold little cell as she wrote," commented the hard-nosed reporter, not given to sentimentalities.

Fr. Coughlin proved to be just as hard-nosed in resisting an interview by the reporter. So Eddie told the saint he admired: "All right lady! If you really are all you're supposed to be, get me this story!" The very next morning he "accidentally" met an old friend who was also a good friend of Fr. Coughlin. A meeting was arranged. Eddie chided Fr. Coughlin for not showing greater consideration to a black sheep, who had not practiced his faith for years. Fr. Coughlin retaliated by refusing to give him the story until he came back to the sacraments. He did, as best he could at the time, and was eventually completely reconciled with God. He went on to become a dedicated lay apostle, and co-founder of Madonna House with his wife Baroness Catherine de Hueck, and was eventually ordained a priest.

Another journalist who had lost his health and his faith read *Story of a Soul*. "Over its pages," says Michael Williams, "it did what no other book caused me to do in all my life before — I wept. Again and again a blinding rush of tears blurred my sight and stopped my reading." When he experienced a sweet fragrance, he presumed the book had been lying near a bottle of perfume. But later, as he entered his apartment, "instantaneously, the breath from Heaven breathed once more upon me. I remembered that the accounts of Sister Thérèse's manifestations are full of such instances of psychic odors." He came back to the Church and for several decades thereafter he was the dean of American Catholic journalists.

These are but a few examples of the great impact this Autobiography of St. Thérèse has had on many thousands of souls, and will have on future generations; for like all true spiritual classics, this book will endure until time is no more. — *The Editor*

"When I am preparing for Holy Communion, I picture my soul as a piece of land and I beg the Blessed Virgin to remove from it *any rubbish* that would prevent it from being *free;* then I ask her to set up a huge tent worthy of *heaven*, adorning it with *her own* jewelry; finally, I invite all the angels and saints to come and conduct a magnificent concert there." —St. Thérèse of the Child Jesus and the Holy Face

St. Thérèse: Light in the Culture of Death

Susan Muldoon, OCDS

Today, death itself is advocated as the ultimate means to escape suffering. Death to the child in the womb is promoted as the answer to the suffering of the mother. Assisted suicide is encouraged as a relief for those enduring the very real pains and anxieties of life. And even those who have spent many years in the spiritual life may wrongfully look for death to take them from the dark night. How insistent are the temptations to take some addictive drug or even take one's life! And how very persuasive the tempter can be if we do not believe in a good God who loves us!

Suffering is essentially a mystery allowed in the Providence of God. God has taught us what we need to know about suffering through His Son, His Church, Sacred Scripture and His saints. St. Thérèse, as a Doctor of the Church, illuminates this mystery for all, including those who advocate the culture of death. In her brief but intense life, St. Thérèse endured many kinds of suffering, most of them hidden from others. She harbored no illusions about suffering, being neither a stoic nor a romantic. Let us allow her to escort us away from the culture of death and despair toward the road of hope leading to eternal life. In the company of Thérèse, let us take a new look at some of the temptations commonly encountered along the path of suffering and death.

Suffering seems interminable and unbearable. In mid-August, a month before her death, Thérèse said, "Oh! how necessary it is to pray for the dying! If you only knew! I believe the demon has asked God permission to tempt me with an extreme suffering, to make me fail in patience and faith. . . . Ah! to suffer in my soul, yes, I can suffer much. . . .But as to suffering of body, I'm like a little child, very little. I'm without any thought, I suffer from minute to minute. . .Never would I have believed it was possible to suffer so much!" Yet, she adds, ". . .all passes away. . .our life of years gone by is past. . .death will also pass. . ."

Every mother knows the exhaustion and seeming endlessness of the pains of labor and birth. But, "When a woman is in travail she has sorrow because her hour has come; but when she is delivered of the child, she no longer remembers the anguish, for joy that a child is born into the world." (Jn 16:21). Suffering is not endless. The truth is that no agony on earth lasts forever.

If we live only by the grace given to us each moment, temptations to despair will not have much power over us. Despair can more easily get a grip on us if we live in anxiety over the future. Thérèse teaches us how to remain poor in spirit and not hold onto our ideas and fears about the future. She spent no time worrying about tomorrow, instead living today as if it were the only day in which to live in God's love with all her attention fixed on Him. "So you have sorrow now, but I will see you again and your hearts will rejoice, and no one will take your joy from you." (Jn 16:22),

"You will have no trouble in loving the Cross and the tears of Jesus if you think often of this saying: 'He loved me and He gave Himself up for me!' . . . How good God really is! How He parcels out trials only according to the strength He gives us. Never would I have been able to bear even the thought of the bitter pains the future held in store for me."

St. Thérèse, who died of tuberculosis, had great difficulty breathing as her illness progressed. This was hard for others to see, but she reassured them, "Don't be disturbed; if I can't breathe, God will give me the strength to bear it. I love Him! He'll never abandon me!. . . .Last night I couldn't take it anymore; I begged the Blessed Virgin to hold my head in her hands so that I could take my sufferings."

Death is a frightening unknown; better to control it by ending it myself. Thérèse did not try to understand everything, but like a child, rested in her mother's arms. The unknown worries us only if we think we must be able to figure it out and live through it alone. The apprehension of a mother anticipating the birth of her first child is similar to one's fear of death. St. Thérèse said, "Someone told me I shall fear death. This could very well be true. There isn't anyone here more mistrustful of her feelings than I am. . . . I know how weak I am. However, I want to rejoice in the feeling that God gives me at the present moment. There will always be time to suffer the opposite."

Thérèse reached the end of her way of the cross like a tired traveler staggering at the end of a long journey: "It is into God's arms that I'm falling!. . . I am not afraid of what happens after death; that is certain! I don't regret giving up my life; but I ask myself: 'What is this mysterious separation of the soul from the body?' It is the first time that I have experienced this, but I abandoned myself immediately to God." St. Thérèse was even tempted to end her life. "Watch carefully, Mother, when you will have patients a prey to violent pains; don't leave any medicines near them that are poisonous. I assure you, it needs only a second when one suffers intensely to lose one's reason. Then one would easily poison oneself. . .What a grace it is to have faith! If I had not any faith, I would have committed suicide without an instant's hesitation."

How to prepare for death? Instead of trying to control her journey, Thérèse waited for Jesus to come for her. "Even now when You [God] join exterior suffering to the trials of my soul, I cannot say: 'The agonies of death have surrounded me', but I cry out in my gratitude: 'I have descended into the valley of the shadow of death, nevertheless, I fear no evil because You are with me, Lord!'. . .All God asks is your good will. From the top of the stairway He is watching you with love. Soon, won over by your useless efforts, He will come down Himself and taking you in His arms will carry you up forever into His kingdom where you will never be separated from Him. . .I abandon myself to what Jesus sees fit to do. . ."

The healthy novice standing at the foot of the crucifix in the Carmelite cloister, where she and her novices threw rose petals, in less than eight years lay dying in the above bed. After her death she began her shower of roses from heaven.

Suffering is useless; why prolong it and be a burden to others?
The world tells us that suffering is totally useless. But deep in our
hearts, we know that there must be some value in it, even in our own
lives. Those of us who have been taught the value of suffering have a
duty to help bear the suffering of others "On earth there will always
be some little cloud since life cannot go on without it, and since in
heaven alone joy will be perfect. However, I desire that as much as
possible God may spare those whom I love the inevitable sufferings
of life, even if it means taking upon myself, if necessary, the trials He
is reserving for them." On the Church's teaching on the Communion
of Saints the *Catechism of the Catholic Church* states ". . . what each
one does or suffers in and for Christ bears fruit for all." Thérèse
shows us how to live this consoling doctrine even in the most obscure
situations. She helps us to listen to the quiet voice of hope rather
than the clamorous voice of despair.

**No one cares that I am suffering, alone and deserted; why should
I continue living?** The example of Mother Teresa of Calcutta has
reminded us all how evil it is to leave the suffering to die alone. How
many die in despair because they do not see any sign of God's love,
whether they are lying in the streets of Calcutta or are in the most
modern medical facility or even in their own homes? The teaching of
Jesus and the example of His saints makes it clear to us that no one
must be abandoned. And yet it is true that in suffering, no matter
how charitably we are cared for, we will ultimately bear suffering
alone. It is not honest to pretend otherwise. Let's listen to the way
St. Thérèse speaks of this aspect of suffering: "[Jesus] alone understands. . . . He alone arranges the events of our life of exile. It is He
who offers us at times the bitter chalice. But we do not see Him; He
is hiding. He veils His divine hand, and we can see only creatures.
Then we suffer since the voice of our Beloved does not make itself
heard and that of creatures seems to misunderstand us. . . in His love
He chooses for His spouses the same road He chose for Himself. . .
He wills that the purest joys be changed into sufferings so that not
having, so to speak, even the time to breathe at ease, our heart may
turn to Him who alone is our Sun and our joy. . ."

Another time, St. Thérèse wrote to her sister Céline about suffering alone: "I am not surprised that you understand nothing that is
taking place . . . .A LITTLE child all alone on the sea, in a boat lost
in the midst of the stormy waves, could she know whether she is close
or far from port? [But] the boat carrying her is advancing with full
sails toward the port, and the rudder which Céline cannot even see is

not without a pilot. Jesus is there, sleeping as in days gone by, . . .But how can He be happy while His spouse is suffering, while she watches during the time He is sleeping. . .? Does He not know that Céline sees only the night, that His divine face remains hidden from her, and even at times the weight she feels on her heart seems heavy to her?. . . What a mystery! And nevertheless Jesus is happy to see her in suffering. He is happy to receive all from her during the night. . . .He is awaiting the dawn and then, oh, then, what an awakening will be the awakening of Jesus!!! Be sure, dear Céline, that your boat is on the open sea, already perhaps very close to port."

St. Thérèse willingly shared the bread of unbelievers and so experienced a double suffering. She knew firsthand the temptation of disbelief coupled with great physical pain. "Your child [Thérèse]. . . O Lord, has understood Your divine light, and she begs pardon for her brothers. She is resigned to eat the bread of sorrow as long as You desire it; she does not wish to rise up from this table filled with bitterness at which poor sinners are eating until the day set by You. . . May all those who were not enlightened by the bright flame of faith one day see it shine." This solidarity does not remove suffering, but helps to make it endurable by encouraging the sufferer to turn from his own pain to look at the Lord and at others. There are many hidden souls on earth who spiritually accompany those who are alone and suffering.

What is the use of suffering if I can't bear it with dignity? The slogan "death with dignity" is often used today, but with a false meaning. True dignity comes from our being created in the image and likeness of God our Father. Accordingly, we read in the *Catechism of the Catholic Church*, "Every human person, created in the image of God, has the natural right to be recognized as a free and responsible being. All owe to each other this duty of respect."(See No. 1738) There is not a person on earth, in whatever miserable or evil circumstances, who does not possess this God-given dignity. The circumstances of suffering and death do not rob a person of this dignity. Being unwanted by others, having a contagious or disfiguring disease, being mentally handicapped or ill, being paralyzed, being addicted to drugs, being falsely accused or mistreated, or living an immoral life does not erase this dignity. It is true that some aspects of life, especially those associated with being sick and dying, do not seem very "dignified." But it is man created in God's image and loved by Him from all eternity who brings dignity to undignified circumstances.

Even in small things, St. Thérèse was not upset to be found imperfect. She did not have a false image of strength and "dignity" to keep up. Instead, she loved to be what she was: little, poor, and dependent on God at every moment. Thinking of the wish of some to suffer with "dignity" and courage, St. Thérèse said we should not want to suffer in a grand manner, but rather aspire to be like Jesus who in an agony sweat blood, was spat upon, scourged and mocked, who fell repeatedly on the dirty ground, was stripped and crucified. "The Blessed Virgin held her dead Jesus on her knees, and He was disfigured, covered with blood! . . . Ah! I don't know how she stood it!"

"To surrender to love is to surrender to all kinds of sufferings," St. Thérèse would say. Of course not all of Thérèse's life was painful. There were happy times as well as painful difficulties of childhood which she admits to having suffered. But these wounds opened her up to Love so that she was to live no longer for herself but for Jesus. Love drew her into Carmel and eventually into the murky darkness and aridity of soul that was to envelop her last eighteen months of life. "[Jesus] permitted my soul to be invaded by the thickest darkness. . . .

"When I want to rest my heart fatigued by the darkness which surrounds it by the memory of the luminous country after which I aspire, my torment redoubles; it seems to me that the darkness, borrowing the voice of sinners, says mockingly to me: 'You are dreaming about the light, about a fatherland embalmed in the sweetest perfumes; you are dreaming about the *eternal* possession of the Creator of all these marvels; you believe that one day you will walk out of this fog which surrounds you! Advance, advance; rejoice in death which will give you not what you hope for but a night still more profound, the night of nothingness'. . . . Ah! may Jesus pardon me if I have caused Him any pain, but He knows very well that while I do not have the *joy of faith*, I am trying to carry out its works at least." She goes on to say: "When I sing of the happiness of heaven and of the eternal possession of God, I feel no joy in this, for I sing simply WHAT I WANT TO BELIEVE."

"I desire no longer either suffering or death, and still I love them both; it is love alone that attracts me. . .abandonment alone guides me. I have no other compass! I can no longer ask for anything with fervor except the accomplishment of God's will in my soul without any creature being able to set obstacles in the way. I can speak these words of The Spiritual Canticle of St. John of the Cross: '. . . After I have known it / LOVE works so in me / That whether things go well or badly / Love turns all to one sweetness / Transforming the soul into itself.'"

What was the key to Thérèse's understanding of suffering? She lived with the simplicity of a child, poor in spirit, full of unshakable confidence in the merciful love of God. The way of spiritual childhood is open to everyone, especially those who are experiencing suffering and temptations that they cannot understand or remove. She once said, "I really count on not remaining inactive in heaven. My desire is to work still for the Church and for souls. I am asking God for this and I am certain He will answer me."

> Holy Mary, Mother of God,
> pray for us sinners,
> now and at the hour of our death. Amen.

"Yes, my Lord, anything You wish, but have mercy on me!...Yes, I think that I have never looked for anything but the truth. Yes, I have understood humility of heart."

Hidden Meaning of the Shower of Roses

The use of roses and rose petals in the life and writings of St. Thérèse is usually associated with her promise of sending a shower of roses (favors) from Heaven after her death to those seeking her help. Indeed, that is the popular and common impression, and with good reason for Pope Puis XI called her a "prodigy of miracles." But there is much deeper symbolism of roses and rose petals in the life of St. Thérèse. True, she would throw rose petals at the feet of the crucifix in the Carmelite garden and encourage her novices to do likewise. But what is the connection between that and the roses (favors) she would let fall from Heaven?

From childhood on, Thérèse had a love for roses and so it was a natural symbolism which she used in expressing a deep theological and spiritual reality. Recognizing that God was not calling her to great visible works such as preaching the Gospel or laying down her life for the Faith, she asked herself, how will I show my love, since love is proven through charitable acts? In her own words she answers: "I have no other means of proving my love for You [Jesus] than that of strewing flowers, that is, not allowing one little sacrifice to escape, not one look, one word, profiting by all the smallest things and doing them through love. . . . and in this way I shall strew flowers before Your throne. I shall not come upon one without plucking off the petals for You . . . .O Jesus, of what use will my flowers be to You?"

"Ah! I know very well that this fragrant shower, these fragile, worthless petals, these songs of love from the littlest of hearts will charm You. Yes, these nothings will please You. They will bring a smile to the Church Triumphant. She will gather up my flowers unpetalled *through love* and have them pass through Your own divine hands, O Jesus. And this Church in heaven desirous of playing with her little child, will cast these flowers, which are now infinitely valuable because of Your divine touch, upon the Church Suffering in order to extinguish its flames and upon the Church Militant in order to gain victory for it!"

So the petals and roses symbolized the many acts of charity and sacrifices, for the most part hidden, that she offered to please Jesus.

Through these "nothings" that she so heroically offered day in and day out in every circumstance, in the dark night of the soul, in the great test of faith, in indescribable sufferings, were the ultimate reason explaining how she could spend her Heaven doing good upon earth as she predicted. She was able to say in her last agonizing days on earth: "I have always given the Good God nothing but love. It is with love He shall repay me. After my death I shall let fall a shower of roses. I shall not rest till the end of the world. I shall spend my Heaven doing good upon earth."

The shower of roses she promised her devotees began shortly after her death on September 30, 1897. A nun who had long suffered from cerebral anemia knelt and leaned her head against the coffin to beg forgiveness for showing impatience with Thérèse on one occasion and was immediately and completely cured. A few days later a new confessor, Abbe Hodierne, granted the community an unheard of favor in those days — which Thérèse had predicted she would obtain: the privilege of daily Communion according to the concession granted by Leo XIII in 1890.

Sister Marie of the Trinity relates how her former novice mistress answered her prayer in a miraculous way but at the same time giving a warning to her former charge. "For the sake of convenience, I had made a large pleat in my habit so that I would not have to adjust it every morning when I put my cincture on. It was firmly sewn with a lock stitch. I told the Servant of God about this a few days before she died, and she told me to unstitch it, that it was contrary to our custom. I left it as it was nevertheless, putting off the job of unstitching it till some other time. The day after her death I could not get this blessed pleat out of my mind. I said to myself: "She sees I still have it, and maybe it grieves her." So, I said this prayer to her: "Dear sister, if you find this pleat displeasing, undo it yourself, and I promise never to remake it." Imagine my amazement when on getting up the following morning I found it was no longer there! My feelings were a mixture of terror and consolation. It was a warning to me to put all her counsels and recommendations into practice."

Seven years after her death, so many miracles and apparitions of the Little Flower were reported to so many people in so many languages, and places that the Bishop of Lisieux had to open the "ordinary" process, the first step towards her eventual canonization. Of the multitude of cures attributed to her, two were scrutinized and accepted for her beatification. The first was the cure of a seminarian dying of tuberculosis. He clutched her relic and demanded, "I didn't come here to die. I came to work for God. You must cure me." She did. The second was the cure of a nun dying of a stomach ulcer. The Little Flower appeared to her and said, "Be generous with God. I promise you will soon be cured." A famous Parisian surgeon wrote a paper to prove the supernatural character of her cure.

At the beatification of the Venerable Thérèse Martin in St. Peter's Basilica, April 29, 1923, someone made the mistake of intoning a *Te Deum*, which is normally reserved for canonization ceremonies. The providential mistake proved to be a prelude for her canonization and title of "wonder worker." For on that day thirty remarkable cures were reported from all over the world. Two of these were selected for scrutiny and were approved for her canonization in 1925.

When the Vice Postulator of her cause, Fr. Roger de Teil, was asked what was necessary to go ahead with the process of canonization, he answered, "Money and miracles," and added "Sister Thérèse is providing us with plenty of both." Up until 1911 the Carmel received about fifty letters daily. Soldiers read her book on both sides of No Man's Land, and dubbed her Little Sister of the Trenches. After 1914, letters were averaging 500 a day. Pius XI called her "a hurricane of glory."

On May 17, 1925, when Pope Pius XI celebrated the Canonization Mass of St. Thérèse before 50,000 inside the basilica and 200,000 outside in the piazza he mentioned in his homily, "We have proof that on entering Paradise she began at once her work among souls." And the Pontiff added, "We see the mystical shower of roses which God permitted her, and still permits her to let fall upon the earth, as she had ingeniously foretold."

As if to confirm what the Holy Father said, high above the main altar, surrounded by a cluster of lights and roses, a picture of the Saint showering roses from Heaven was displayed. A most remarkable incident occurred. Suddenly as the Holy Father ended his homily, five roses detached themselves from the floral display and floated down in a wide spiral for all to see, and landed right at his feet. In a sense it wasn't remarkable, since anyone familiar with St. Thérèse knows how frequently she sends roses to indicate her presence, or as a sign assuring her petitioners that their prayers were heard.

As mentioned above, there were a number of instances in which St. Thérèse appeared to people after her death. One extraordinary instance which is rather humorous happened on the night of January 16, 1910. The Mother Prioress of the Carmel of Gallipoli, Italy, wrote the following to the Prioress of Lisieux:

"I felt very ill and was preoccupied with our grave financial difficulties. About three o'clock in the morning, I sensed in my sleep a hand adjust my blanket with tender care. I thought one of my sisters came to help me in my distress, so I told her without opening my eyes: 'Please let me alone, I am perspiring profusely.' But a sweet unknown voice replied: 'No, I want to do you a favor. Listen, the good Lord makes use of the citizens of Heaven, as of people on earth, to help His servants. I have 500 francs which you will be able to pay the debt of your community. But since you may not keep the money in your cell, come with me.'

"I found myself outside my cell in the company of a young Carmelite Sister whose dress and veil were spreading a kind of celestial light which enabled us to walk in the dark. She led me to the room where a money box was located. It containing nothing but a bill for 300 francs. She deposited 500 francs in the box. I was overjoyed as I watched, then I fell on my knees and exclaimed: 'O my Holy Mother!' But she replied, while helping me to rise with tender affection: 'No, I am not our Holy Mother, I am the Servant of God, Sister Thérèse of Lisieux.' But I was so moved and confused that I exclaimed again, 'O my Mother,' and I was unable to say more as she, putting her hand on my veil in a gesture of sisterly care, withdrew." In telling her community of this extraordinary "dream" the next morning, the Sisters insisted that they look in the money box, and sure enough there was the 500 francs. The Prioress concludes the account: "Our whole community is really confused by the immense goodness of Sister Thérèse."

Today, novenas in her honor have somewhat dwindled, but her Shower of Roses continues, as her clients continue to seek her help (see listing on page 162 of publications that carry the shower of roses she continues to grant her petitioners). Of course, the ultimate reason for the shower of roses is to draw attention to her "Little Way," a sure and easy way to conversion, personal holiness, peace and eternal joy.

—Editor

Sister Geneviève, the photographer of the Lisieux Carmel

St. Thérèse of the Child Jesus

When Céline entered the Lisieux Carmel she brought her camera and paints and brushes to the cloister. We must remember that her camera was not the best available, some of the film plates were defective, others were scratched or damaged when Céline developed and printed. Thérèse had mobile features, and could hold a pose for nine or ten seconds. But it is incredible that she looks like two different persons in photos taken only a few minutes apart. Because of the awkward position of the coffin and the corpse, the photo taken the day after death is out of focus, the face elongated, the eyebrows black instead of blonde. But it is accurate in showing that Thérèse looked about twelve or thirteen years old, with a heavenly smile. In 1905, at the request of many, Céline painted the famous picture of Thérèse in her coffin. The nuns called it a true likeness. The fascinating history of her art is given in Photo Album of St. Thérèse (P. J. Kennedy, N.Y., 1962), see page 160 for ad.

—Fr. Pacificus Kennedy

Part VI

1. St. Francis and St. Thérèse — Spiritual Brother and Sister

Bro. Francis Mary Kalvelage, F.I.

2. Mirror of the Blessed Virgin

Fra. Maximilian Mary, F.I.

3. He Found Mary Through Thérèse

Msgr. Vernon Johnson

4. A Natural Poet with a Message

Joseph Kochiss

Francis of Assisi and Thérèse of Lisieux
Spiritual Brother and Sister

Bro. Francis Mary Kalvelage, F.I.

Judging by their universal popularity and following, there are two saints in the Church calendar who could be said to be epochal and universal saints. They are St. Francis of Assisi and St. Thérèse of Lisieux. Apart from the Blessed Mother, what saints have had the impact on society, culture, arts and spirituality, and continue to have, as have Saints Francis and Thérèse? It should be no surprise then to see some striking similarities between the two. The comparison of St. Thérèse with St. Francis is no more apparent, and rightly so, than in their literal interpretation of the Gospel. They both threw new light on certain passages of the Gospel and based their spirituality upon these passages. Of utmost importance, they lived the Gospels to the hilt.

The study of Scripture was not merely a case of theologizing, as we see so much in our times. To them Scripture was to be known, loved and *lived*. It had to have a practical application in their own lives and spirituality, and in those who would follow them in turning away from sin and seeking personal holiness. In his living what he discovered (or perhaps *recovered* would be a better word for it) St. Francis had an impact on the thirteenth century (the dawn of the modern world) as St. Thérèse has had on our own twentieth century (its sunset) that sets them apart from all other saints.

Unique and different in many ways, but in the essentials the same, the saint of the "Little Way of Spiritual Childhood" and the saint of evangelical poverty, "the Little Poor Man of Assisi," lived centuries apart. One was the founder of a religious order (the Friars Minor as Francis wanted them to be known) the other a hidden, cloistered Carmelite nun. Both, however, had many followers. St. Francis founded a religious order that has existed for over 750 years and has had many followers, both men and women religious as well as lay people, many of whom are canonized saints. In the case of St. Thérèse, how can one tabulate the number of souls who have followed her "little way of spiritual childhood"? It numbers many millions, judging by the many editions and translations of *Story of a Soul*. How can one assess the number and the tremendous influence in our times of the legion of little "victim souls" consecrated to God's Merciful Love that St. Thérèse begged of Jesus? Both saints were totally given to the love of God and winning souls who would love Him and glorify Him for all eternity.

St. Francis and St. Thérèse were called to great things, and they knew it. In the case of St. Thérèse we see how she envisioned her place among the greats though she ever strove in this life to be forgotten and trodden underfoot like a grain of sand. In the lives of St. Francis written by early biographers they practically all agree that he was destined for great things even before he discovered his calling to renew the Church which, as Christ pointed out, was falling into ruins. As a young man he went off to battle, to win fame and his place among the knights of his day in a war with a neighboring city-state, only to end up a prisoner of war with other POWs. They were imprisoned in a damp, cold dungeon with little light. His fellow sufferers were near to despair after a year. But Francis, joking about their misfortune, lifted their spirits with his good humor and crazy ways. They couldn't understand how he could be joyful

Both Saints had an intense love and loyalty to the Church. Francis is often referred to as "*the* Catholic man," thoroughly Catholic, and willing to die for the faith. Neither became bloody martyrs for the faith, but rather both were martyrs of seraphic love.

under the circumstances. He even boasted, "I see the day when all the world will bow before me." Recall how Thérèse also envisioned the day when the whole world would be attracted to her and her "Little Way."

Her "Little Way" (as explained in the article on page 2) is nothing else but returning to Holy Scripture in all its fundamental truth and simplicity. St. Thérèse took literally the passage from the Gospel: "Unless you become as little children you shall not enter the Kingdom of God" (Matt 18: 14) and drew from it a spirituality that revolutionized the spiritual lives of millions. St. Francis too turned to the Gospel when he strove to find out what God wanted of him and his followers. Already enamored with his "Lady Poverty," when he heard the Gospel of the Mass of February 24, 1209 in which Christ was sending his apostles out to preach the good news, "Do not possess gold, nor silver, nor money in your purses: no scribe for your journey, nor two coats, nor shoes, nor staff. . ."(Matt 10: 9-10) he exclaimed joyfully, "That is what I seek, what I desire with all my heart!"

When Francis wrote his rule of life he declared unequivocally, "The Most High Himself revealed to me that I should live according to the form of the holy Gospel. And I caused it to be written in few words and simple and the Lord Pope confirmed it for me." Thus we have St. Francis in the thirteenth century returning to the simplicity of the Gospel in a literal interpretation of a life of poverty as lived by Christ and His holy Mother, and St. Thérèse in the nineteenth century uncovering and living a passage of the Gospel that had not been fully developed and articulated. In the words of our Holy Father, Pope John Paul II, when he visited her shrine in Lisieux in 1980: "Thérèse reminds us that the most fundamental and most universal truth of the Gospel message is that God is our Father and we are His children."

In a society that has lost sight of this truth through its self centeredness and materialism, along comes a young twenty-four-year-old to teach the "wise and the prudent" of this world the truth that, indeed, we have a heavenly Father from whom all love and mercy descends to His creatures, through His Son, Jesus Christ. In an era which is stuck in the mire of materialism which leaves little room for the virtue of hope, the Holy Spirit did raise up a saint to meet the crisis of the times.

Seven hundred years before, in the times of St. Francis, the mercantile class was slowly emerging, which eventually would be the "haves" of our day. Francis chose to be identified with the Minors, the "have nots" of his day, over the Majors, the "haves" (nobility). Coming from the family of a rich cloth merchant, he was inspired to counteract the emerging worldliness and secularism of his day, which has reached its peak in our day in the "culture of death." Francis, in his utter detachment of creatures and total attachment to the Creator, met head-on the acquisitiveness of men to seek wealth and power rather than God; to be attached to this world rather than set one's eyes on eternity and heaven.

Thérèse taught the same message of Gospel literalness (simplicity and single-mindedness) and "littleness" (humility) as Francis. Her message of "spiritual childhood" moreover is tailored for our times, with its highly sophisticated, overrated institutions of higher learning, but which are spiritually undernourished and impoverished. In raising up little Thérèse as the greatest saint and religious mover of our twentieth century, God disdained the highly educated, for this French girl had few years of formal education (attention home schooling parents!). Though she had no trouble in expressing herself in the most straightforward, interesting, and at times lyrical ways, she wasn't constrained with accidentals (such as good spelling) when eternal truths were to be articulated. Her life was short and time was in short supply in the Carmel of Lisieux (maybe dictionaries too).

They both had an intense love and loyalty to the Church. Francis is often referred to as "*the* Catholic man," thoroughly Catholic, and willing to die for the faith. This desire for martyrdom is seen in his going into the heart of the Saracen empire to convert the Sultan Malek-al-Khamil. St. Thérèse, a young girl of fourteen visiting the coliseum in Rome, kissed the ground where the Christians were martyred, asking God to grant this grace to her. Neither became bloody martyrs for the faith, but rather both were martyrs of seraphic love. Francis of Assisi, inflamed with a consuming love of the God made man in the poverty at Bethlehem, the rejected and crucified Savior and his total self abnegation in the Eucharist, is widely known as the "Seraphic Saint." The highest choir of angels, the nearest to God are the seraphim; and who would deny the same title of "Seraphic Saint" to Thérèse of the Holy Face who made her whole life a Holocaust to God's Merciful Love?

The two characteristic Loves which both were noted for were love of Jesus and Mary. Francis attributed the founding of his order to the inspiration of Mary. When Francis came to die, he asked to be brought to the little church of St. Mary of the Angels: there the Order had its beginnings, there Our Lady had appeared to him and it was there that he wished to die. He was the first to speak of Our Lady as the "Spouse of the Holy Spirit," seeing the intimate relationship between her and the Holy Spirit. In our own day, the Franciscan devotee of St. Thérèse, St. Maximilian Kolbe, carried Francis' title and perennial Franciscan devotion to the Immaculate Conception one step further in developing the concept of the

Holy Spirit as the "uncreated Immaculate Conception."

The love and filial devotion that St. Thérèse had to the Blessed Mother is on practically every page of her writings. We see this from the time that she was six years old, when she wrote, "I want to be a very good little girl. The Blessed Virgin is my dear Mother and little children usually resemble their mother." Among the last words she put on paper before she died at twenty-four were: "Mary, if I were the Queen of Heaven and you were Thérèse, I should want to be Thérèse that you might be the Queen of Heaven. . . .We are happier than she is for she has not the Blessed Virgin to love, and that is a happiness we have that she has not! Oh how I love the Blessed Virgin!" (More on this in the chapter on page 119.)

The total love of both Saints for Jesus was never more visible and apparent than in the faith and love they had in, of and for Jesus present in the Eucharist. Francis would cry out pitifully: "The God of love is not loved!" Jesus' Real Presence was the focus of the whole life of Francis. "In this world," Francis points out, "I cannot see the most high Son of God with my own eyes, except for His most holy Body and Blood in the Eucharist." With awe and wonder he would say: "What wonderful majesty! . . . That the Lord of the whole universe, God and the Son of God, should humble Himself like this and hide under the form of a little bread, for our salvation."

St. Thérèse's devotion to the Eucharist is brought out in other chapters, especially "Mystical Simplicity" (page 7). We find in her writings frequent references to her consuming desire to be one with Jesus and in particular the Eucharistic Jesus. As early as her first Holy Communion she writes, "On the day of my first Communion we were no longer two: Thérèse had disappeared as a drop of water lost in the ocean. Only Jesus remained. He was the Master, the King." She saw His presence in two ways: the Sacrament of transforming union — the ultimate end of all her desires — and in the permanent Real Presence which called for her loving presence in adoration. She very readily associated the hidden, buffeted, defiled face of Jesus with the hidden Jesus in the Eucharist.

Both their lives were impressed with a close identification with Christ, the suffering Servant, the Crucified Christ. Towards the end of St. Francis' life, while he prayed atop of Mt. Alverna, a visible sign of the invisible union with his crucified Lord took place. Francis was marked by the stigmata, the first recorded instance of this great supernatural gift. During a vision of Christ nailed to the cross, the marks of the nails were left in his flesh. His side too had a wound similar to the lance wound that pierced the side of Christ, from which blood frequently flowed.

Although the saint of the "Little Way" did not have the stigmata, in her act of "Oblation to the Merciful Love of God," she petitioned God: "Since You deigned to give me a share in this precious Cross, I hope in heaven to resemble You and to see shining in my glorified body the sacred Stigmata of Your Passion." It has never been recorded that Our Lady had the visible wounds of her Divine Son in her chaste body, but her compassion in seeing her son die in agony and in desolation was a far greater suffering than the physical suffering which could have offered her some relief, in as much as she would be thus sharing in His passion. So too in the last year of her life when she went through the desolation of the crucified Christ, seemingly abandoned by the Father, Thérèse heroically bore a suffering which in some ways was greater than the stigmata.

Although (or because) their lives were filled with great suffering, which they never avoided but embraced as redemptive, they were filled with peace and joy. One has but to recall the "Perfect Joy" of St. Francis as related in the *Little Flowers of St. Francis.* St. Thérèse expressed that same joy in these words from *Story of a Soul*: "True wisdom consists in 'desiring to be unknown and counted as nothing,' in 'placing one's joy in the contempt of self.' Ah! I desired that, like the Face of Jesus, 'my face be truly hidden, that no one on earth would know me.' I thirsted after suffering and I longed to be forgotten."

Nearing death one night with unspeakable pains, St. Francis' usual cheerfulness threatened to leave him. He was consoled by an interior voice that told him to rejoice and trust so confidently as if he were already in the Father's kingdom. The following morning he composed the immortal hymn of praise and joy, the "Canticle of the Sun." In those last painful days and nights, he asked his brothers to sing again and again this hymn of praise of all God's creation. Reproached by one of his brothers that this preparation for death might offend others, he answered smilingly:

"Permit me, brother, to rejoice in the Lord and in His praise and my own infirmities, since by the grace of the Holy Spirit I am so united and joined to the Lord that by His mercy I may well rejoice greatly in Him." Is not St. Thérèse's abandonment to God's Merciful Love an echo of this?

In conclusion, this cursory coverage, showing the intimate relationship between the two saints, could easily be expanded into a book. A whole chapter could be devoted to their great reverence and appreciation of the priesthood (see article on page 73) though neither belonged to the ministerial priesthood. But the essential point is their reproducing Christ's life in their lives. St. Francis is recognized by all Christians as the one who most perfectly imitated the Savior in his life. He is often referred to as the mirror of Christ. But who would question that the perfect imitator of Christ in the practice of virtue and in reflecting His love of God and fellow man, is the Blessed Virgin Mary? Even as St. Francis was the most perfect replica of Christ, a good case could be made for St. Thérèse perfectly replicating the virtues and hidden life of the Blessed Virgin for our times, the age of Mary.

The painting of St. Thérèse in the center of Bernini's "window of the Holy Spirit" in St. Peter's Basilica which was unveiled for her Beatification.

Mirror of the Blessed Virgin

Fra Maximilian Mary, F.I.

In celebrating the centenary of St. Thérèse of Lisieux, we honor "Papa God" who formed His little daughter into a replica of God's masterpiece, Mary Immaculate. At age six Thérèse wrote, "I want to be a very good girl. The Blessed Virgin is my dear Mother and little children usually resemble their mother." Thérèse became, as it were, an extension of the Blessed Virgin by her perfect imitation of her virtues. It is precisely Mary's hidden virtues, her ordinary life at Nazareth, which are echoed in the life and writings of St. Thérèse whose life and writings were Marian from beginning to end.

However, unlike Mary, Thérèse was born with Original Sin. The Immaculate Conception sets Mary apart from all God's creatures. Thus, we may be tempted to feel estranged from her. Not so St. Thérèse. She would say that she was more blessed being Thérèse than Mary, because then she could love and admire Mary, whom she recognized as "more Mother than Queen." Thérèse seems to "borrow" from the theology of how Mary could be immaculately conceived and still be redeemed when, speaking of herself, Thérèse writes, ". . . Jesus has *forgiven me more* than *St. Mary Magdalene* since He forgave me *in advance* by preventing me from falling. I was preserved from it only through God's mercy!" Applying this to Our Lady: unlike the rest of men who are conceived in original sin, she received the greatest possible mercy, the perfect redemption, freedom from sin at the moment of her conception in anticipation of her Son's redemptive death. Like Mary, Thérèse considered this preventive mercy a precious gift. When she made a general confession of her whole life in her first months in Carmel her confessor "spoke the most consoling words I ever heard in my life: *'In the presence of God, the Blessed Virgin, and all the Saints, I DECLARE THAT YOU HAVE NEVER COMMITTED A MORTAL SIN.* . . . Thank God for what He has done for you.' . . . and gratitude flooded my soul."

From the moment of her Conception the Heart of Mary was ever perfectly conformed to God's Will. She always said "Yes" to God. At the Annunciation when Gabriel revealed God's plan for her and the world,

119

she uttered her *"Fiat"* to the singular grace of being the Mother of God. "Behold the handmaid of the Lord: be it done to me according to thy word." (Lk 1:38). In her autobiography Thérèse writes that from the age of three on, she refused God nothing. She desired to become a saint, a great saint. She explains this great desire of her life in the incident when as a child of four she "chose all." In the "Story of a Soul" she writes: "This little incident of my childhood is a summary of my whole life; later on when perfection was set before me. . . I cried out 'My God *I choose all! I* don't want to be a *saint by halves. I'm* not afraid to suffer for You, I fear only one thing: to keep my *own will*; so take it, for *I choose all* that You will!"

The fruit of union with the divine Will is union with God Himself. For our Blessed Mother this union was most perfect and fruitful — within her womb the "Word was made flesh and dwelt among us." (Jn 1:14). He whom all the heavens and earth could not contain emptied Himself and, with ineffable humility and love, rejoiced to be encompassed within the womb of Mary. What a marvel! It was especially in Holy Communion that Thérèse partook of this profound and astonishing union with the Word made flesh. "It is not to remain in a golden ciborium that He comes to us *each day* from Heaven; it's to find another heaven," she writes, "infinitely more dear to Him than the first: the heaven of our soul, made in His image, the living temple of the adorable Trinity!"

In her union with the eucharistic Jesus, Thérèse particularly desired to be adorned with Mary's virtues. In fact, she realized that to be most pleasing to Jesus one must become like the Blessed Mother in such a way that, as she wrote to Mary, "when the white Host comes into my heart,/ Jesus, your Sweet Lamb, thinks He is resting in you!" (v.5) She calls this sacramental union a "fusion" where "all the joy of Heaven. . . entered my heart." It was a time of loving exchange between her soul and God. It was a time "to be His living temple" like the Virgin of Nazareth at the Annunciation.

When Jesus became present in Mary's womb, she went with haste to bring Christ to John the Baptist in the womb of Elizabeth. It was during that Spirit-filled greeting that Mary sang her canticle of love to the Almighty. He so delighted in her lowliness that He chose her among all women. Singularly blessed, she magnified the Lord and rejoiced in God her Savior. She acknowledged that God exalts the lowly, feeds the hungry, and shows mercy on those who reverently fear Him. (cf. Lk 1:46 ff.)

In the opening lines of her "Story of a Soul" Thérèse indicates the "one thing" she intends to do in heaven: "I shall begin to sing what I must sing eternally: *The Mercies of the Lord."* Her writings and her entire earthly life can be described as a personalized *Magnificat* which shall never end. She explains "that the Almighty has done great things in the soul of His divine Mother's child [Thérèse], and the greatest thing is to have shown her *littleness*, her impotence." Precisely because of this littleness she sought a way to be lifted up to God. "I wanted to find an elevator which would raise me to Jesus, for I am too small to climb the rough stairway of perfection . . . . The elevator which must raise me to Heaven is Your arms, O Jesus! And for this I had no need to grow up, but rather I had to remain *little* and become this more and more."

Mary "rejoices" in God, her Savior. She walked always in that "unspeakable and triumphant joy" (1 Pt 1:8) which the world cannot give or take away. She is rightly called the Cause of Our Joy. Thérèse too was overflowing with this supernatural joy. She records how she gained the good graces of the old and infirm Sr. St. Pierre, who "was not easy to please," by her many acts of charity and because "I gave her my most beautiful smile. . . ." There is something about a genuine smile which by its self-forgetfulness and love softens even the hardest of hearts and heals the deepest of wounds.

Moreover, it was "Our Lady of the Smile" who miraculously healed her at the age of ten. She was so sick with a mysterious illness that there was little hope of recovery. In desperation three of her sisters, kneeling before the statue of Mary, pleaded for their sister, when "all of a sudden the Blessed Virgin appeared *beautiful* to me, so *beautiful* that never had I seen anything so attractive; her face was suffused with an ineffable benevolence and tenderness, but what penetrated to the very depths of my soul was the *'ravishing smile of the Blessed Virgin.'*"

Mary's life was inseparable from Jesus' and her Immaculate Heart was ever fixed on pleasing Him. Though she was the Mother of God, her life was ordinary and hidden — it was made up of *little things*. But the extraordinary faith, hope, and charity which animated her penetrated the heavens. She made and mended clothes for Him who clothes the lilies of the field and who designed the universe. She cooked for Him who feeds the birds of the air and opens wide His hand to feed all in due season. She cleaned the house for Him who alone can cleanse the hearts of men.

Thérèse's life too was steeped in Christ Jesus — everything centered on Him. "I had offered myself, for some time now, to the Child Jesus as His *little plaything* . . . ." she writes. "I wanted to *amuse little Jesus,* to give Him pleasure; I wanted to give myself up to His *childish whims. He heard my prayer.*" The thought of the Child Jesus was ever on her mind and she did the littlest of things with immense love just to please Him. The less noticed the better. Mary washed the clothes of Jesus, and

Thérèse considered herself "very fortunate, to prepare the linens and Sacred vessels destined to come in contact with Jesus."

But authentic devotion to the Child Jesus includes suffering. Can one imagine the pain Mary experienced when Jesus was lost in the temple? Mary Immaculate, who ever exercised perfect maternal love, had lost her Son. She was fully aware that He loved her with the most tender, filial love. This made her all the more vulnerable to the anguish which she was about to undergo. Nothing forewarned her of the overwhelming three days of separation she experienced when Jesus remained in Jerusalem. Her preeminent virtue and His singular love would indicate that such a trial could never happen.

In her poem to Mary, Thérèse probes the depths of this mystery. "Mother, your sweet Child wants you to be an example/ Of the soul searching for Him in the night of faith.// Since the King of Heaven wanted His Mother/ To be plunged into the night, in anguish of heart,/ Mary, is it thus a blessing to suffer on earth?/ Yes, *to suffer while loving is the purest happiness!*" (v.15-16) She writes both from fruitful meditation and personal experience. She was pure, never staining her baptismal robe with mortal sin. Yet God "permitted my soul to be invaded by the thickest darkness. . . .He knows very well that while I do not have *the joy of faith,* I am trying to carry out its works at least." This severe trial of Thérèse's faith lasted for over a year until her death. To the very end she maintained her grateful, generous disposition to suffer for the love of God and the conversion of poor sinners. "Everything is a grace!" she would say in her last days of torment.

"Mary kept in mind all these things pondering them in her heart" (Lk 2:19). Like the Virgin Mary's, Thérèse's very life was a profound prayer, a continual dialogue of love with her Lord and God. She prayed without ceasing and saw God's providential hand in every aspect of her life. For her *"prayer* is an aspiration of the heart, it is a simple glance directed to Heaven, it is a cry of gratitude and love in the midst of trial as well as joy; finally it is something great, supernatural, which expands my soul and unites me to Jesus." Mary, the Mystical Rose, and Thérèse, the Little Flower, each strove for an ever deeper union with Jesus corresponding to the grace bestowed on each of them.

Mary "stood" at the foot of the cross actively cooperating with Jesus Crucified in redeeming the world, and became Mother of the Church and of each of its members. God the Father permitted the sword of sorrow to transfix her Immaculate Heart precisely because He willed that by her compassion she might also be our Coredemptrix and Spiritual Mother. The agonizing spiritual desolation of Jesus on the Cross, "abandoned" by the Father, was experienced by Thérèse, and undoubtedly by the Mother of Sorrows as well. Trials and tribulations were to her the greatest honor the Father could bestow on His child. Each sacrifice was an opportunity to renew her generous love for God and to unleash grace for poor sinners.

She recalls how at the age of 14, "looking at a picture of Our Lord on the Cross, I was struck by the Blood flowing from one of the divine hands. I felt a great pang of sorrow when thinking this Blood was falling to the ground without anyone's hastening to gather it up. I was resolved to remain in spirit at the foot of the Cross and to receive the divine dew. I understood I was then to pour it out upon souls... I offered to God all the infinite merits of Our Lord."

After his victorious death and resurrection, Jesus willed that Mary remain and that her Immaculate Heart be, as it were, the very Heart of the Church. With all the ardor of Her Immaculate Heart, she prayed in the midst of the Apostles at Pentecost. Her Immaculate Heart was an ongoing link to the Incarnation and Redemption. She was in their midst for many years — interceding, instructing, and loving. We cannot begin to understand the depths of divine charity abiding within her Heart. Her zeal for the salvation of souls is limitless, especially for sinners who found in her a Mother of Mercy and Refuge of Sinners.

As mentioned in several other chapters of this book St. Thérèse in her great love of Christ and souls desired all vocations — warrior, priest, apostle, doctor, martyr. "My desires caused me a veritable martyrdom." St. Paul in his first Epistle to the Corinthians opened her mind and heart to realize all her ambitions — charity! ". . . .I understood that the Church *had a Heart and that this Heart* was *BURNING WITH LOVE. I understood it was Love alone* that made the Church's members act. . . .I understood that LOVE COMPRISED ALL VOCATIONS. . . .my *vocation,* at last I have found it. . . . MY VOCATION IS LOVE!. . . in the heart of the Church, my Mother, I shall be *Love.*" Our Lady and our Saint both lived this hidden vocation of love which is so essential to the entire mystical Body of Christ, the Church.

Our Lady's cooperation with Christ the one Mediator is unique and her membership in His mystical Body is preeminent precisely because of her perfect cooperation with every grace He gave her.

"Who is my mother and who is my brethren?. . .Whoever does the will of my Father in Heaven, he is my brother and sister and mother" (Mt 12: 48-50). God has freely chosen to entrust all grace and the entire order of mercy to her. "She is a mother to us in the order of grace. . . Taken up to Heaven she did not lay aside this saving office but by her manifold intercession continues to bring us the gifts of eternal salvation." (Lumen Gentium 61, 62). As Mediatrix of All Grace and Mercy she continues to actively carry out her maternal mission in the hearts and minds of all her children. Similarly, Thérèse realized that her silent, simple hidden life was not only significant, but of prominent importance in the Church. Because God desired her little way to be of great importance for the entire Church, she too has been entrusted a role in Heaven. In her last weeks she revealed, "I feel that my mission is about to begin, my mission of making others love God as I love Him, my mission of teaching my little way to souls . . . . Yes, I want to spend my Heaven in doing good on earth."

How remarkable is the resemblance between Mary and Thérèse, between Mother and child! As the saintly Curè of Ars put it: "Virtue passes readily from the heart of a mother to that of her child." Let us heed the message which St. Thérèse wishes to teach us: only those who are "little" in their own eyes and in the eyes of the world will learn to love and resemble their Mother. Only then will they reach the heights of virtue and union with God to which our Saint attained. We end with her own words addressed to our heavenly Mother:

While waiting for Heaven, O my dear Mother,

I want to live with you, to follow you each day.

Mother, contemplating you, I joyfully immerse myself,

discovering in your Heart *abysses of love...* (v.18)

Unless otherwise noted in the text, all quotes are from "Story of a Soul" or the poem "Why I Love You, O Mary! "(verse indicated)

He Found Mary Through Thérèse

By Msgr. Vernon Johnson

The great apostle of the Spirituality of St. Thérèse, Msgr. Vernon Johnson, like so many Protestant converts (see article on page 78) found devotion to Our Lady incomprehensible. Although attributing his conversion to the reading of "Story of a Soul," at first Msgr. Johnson wasn't that aware of the integral role Mary played in the Little Way of Spiritual Childhood. Shortly after his conversion he went to the famous Beda College in Rome to study for the priesthood. The following is excerpted from a writing of Msgr. Vernon Johnson.

My first few weeks in Rome passed uneventfully until one Sunday, being faced with certain difficulties, I went to my director to ask his counsel. In his reply he said that the one thing which would help me most in this particular problem was an increased devotion to Our Lady and that I must get to know her better. The following day a friend of mine, a convert and an ex-clergyman, asked me to go for a drive with himself and his wife and we arranged to go on the following Thursday.

Meanwhile that Wednesday I was due to lunch with a certain Canon, also a convert from Switzerland. After lunch he took me into the garden and taking my arm he said: "You must forgive me if I am presuming but I have been very interested in your conversion and I have been praying for you for a long time and in my prayer God seems to tell me that I must urge you at all costs to learn more about Our Lady, that you may have a greater devotion to her. You are never safe until you are a true child of Mary. I notice," he said, "that there is no mention of her in your book, *One Lord, One Faith.*"*

"You cannot get this devotion," he continued, "either by merely reading about her or even by merely praying to her. You must visit the shrines hallowed by her appearances and her miracles and you will be forced to

---

*This book, a best seller having twenty-nine editions, with seven translations at the last count, is an apologia Monsignor wrote for his entering the Catholic Church. As a popular speaker and retreat director in the Church of England, he felt it necessary to explain to his many friends and followers why he joined the Church of Rome.

the conclusion either that all these shrines are frauds, which is impossible, or that Our Lady does act miraculously upon human life in a way nobody else does except her Divine Son." He begged me to go to various shrines, especially Genazzano, Italy, and Lourdes. I was a little nettled at the directness of this conversation and rather grudgingly said I would try and do what I could. The following day as we started on our drive I asked "Where are we going?" My friends replied: "We are taking you to Genazzano, the most important shrine of Our Lady in the neighborhood of Rome. The shrine of Our Lady of Good Counsel." I was profoundly startled by what at the least was a very strange coincidence. Here I was, the very day after my Swiss friend had so strongly urged me to visit the shrines of Our Lady, involuntarily doing the very thing which he had urged me to do, through no planning or scheming of my own.

I asked the history of the shrine and was told how the picture had been miraculously transported across the sea. I found it very difficult to believe. Arrived at the shrine, we knelt before the unveiled picture. I prayed to Our Lady: "I don't quite know why you have brought me here but I know that this sanctuary is authorized by Holy Church as a place of devotion and so I beg you to enlighten me." After we had paid our devotion to the shrine we all went into the sacristy to buy medals and souvenirs. I was not very anxious to buy any; my friends, however, handed me a box containing a hundred or more medals of the picture. I put my hand into the box and took a medal and when I looked at it, it was not a medal of Our Lady of Good Counsel but a medal of St. Thérèse! I could hardly believe my eyes.

Then at once it occurred to me that, of course, St. Thérèse gets everywhere and that no doubt they sold her medal as well as various others. I searched through the box but there was not another to be found. I asked the Canon who was in charge and he could not explain it either. By this time I was completely dumbfounded as also were my friends. Granted that the medal had been accidentally dropped into the box by mere human agency, the fact that I with my history should have been the one to pick it out was something more than coincidence.

I began to have that strange feeling which I felt so strongly on my first visit to Lisieux, the sense of an unseen person acting upon me from outside of me, the person of St. Thérèse. That she was somehow connected with my visit to Genazzano was now perfectly clear—at first this was all I could realize. Then as we returned in the car to Rome I began to see that St. Thérèse had given me yet another of her little signs showing me that it was her wish that I should follow the advice of my Swiss friend and visit as many of the shrines of Our Lady as I could. A sign from St. Thérèse is a command from heaven and so I gladly determined to obey—

and then it suddenly became clear how in my study of the Autobiography and the poems of St. Thérèse, by some strange act of Providence, the reality and significance of her devotion to Our Lady had been withheld from my eyes, even though I knew that the one miracle in the life of the Saint was that which was associated with Our Lady's miraculous smile.

I returned once again to St. Thérèse's writings and found, of course, her devotion to Our Lady shining out of almost every page. As a result of this experience I determined to go to Lourdes as soon as I could but unfortunately I had to wait another year before that resolution could be fulfilled. I started on my pilgrimage at the end of the term, intending to lay two problems at the feet of Our Lady at the Grotto of Lourdes. Arriving at Lourdes, I prayed daily at the Grotto and performed many of the customary penances but, so far as I could tell, Our Lady gave me no answer whatever.

Marvelous as was the experience of the pilgrimage, it was with a feeling of disappointment that I left Lourdes for Lisieux where I intended to make my annual visit of thanksgiving. During my stay I made my way as usual to *Les Buissonets*, the home of the Saint which had made such a powerful impression upon me during my first visit. There, as I knelt once more in prayer in the room where St. Thérèse had been so ill and where she had been cured by the miraculous smile of Our Lady, all of a sudden, I realized quite clearly that it was in this room that I received the light, the wound in my soul, the grace of conversion which brought me into the Church. Therefore, I had received the grace of conversion in the very room where St. Thérèse had had her supreme relationship with Our Lady.

In other words I had indeed received my conversion from our Divine Lord, but at the hands of Our Lady and St. Thérèse. How this significant fact had been veiled from my eyes to this day I do not understand. How I had been blind to the importance of the miraculous smile of Our Lady in the life of St. Thérèse and to the depths of the Saint's devotion to our Blessed Mother; and how I had failed to realize that it was in that room that I had received my conversion, all this I simply do not know. I had had to go to Italy to the shrine at Genazzano to find out this simple fact. It was to teach me these facts that I had been led to the shrine of Our Lady of Good Counsel. The meaning of my visit to that shrine and of the medal of St. Thérèse which I found there was now luminous.

Note article on Page 78, *How St. Thérèse Found a Priest-Brother* by Sr. Marie Immanuel, S.C.

A Natural Poet with a Message

Joseph Kochiss

Every holy thought, spoken or written down, by a saint is in a sense a relic of that saint. Such is true of St. Thérèse of the Child Jesus who professed that three minutes would not pass without her thinking of God. This somewhat explains how, in her short life of twenty-four years, she could produce such abundant writings, consisting in over 266 letters (others had not been preserved by the recipient), sixty-two poems, twenty-one prayers, eight plays and her spiritual classic, *Story of a Soul*.

We know Thérèse's life story through her autobiography; but now with new interest focused on her through her being declared a Doctor of the Church, her other writings are being translated for English speaking readers. Her poetry is already available (see page 159) and soon her plays will also be. All her writings reflect the same spiritual message. They complement, expand, and elucidate each other exquisitely. This is especially true of her poetry.

As with her prose, Thérèse had no pretensions of writing poetry seriously. She wrote her verses while in the Carmel for the most part on request. Her poetry displays no grandiose or sophisticated style but rather a simple, clear expression of her devotional thoughts as they naturally flowed from her fertile mind. She concentrates on the person of Christ and her spousal relationship with Him, on Mary, the saints, her family, virtues, spiritual childhood and abandonment to God's Merciful Love. Clearly they confirm, expand and enhance the spiritual message that Thérèse lived and found in her other writings.

Less than six months before she died she confided to her sister Céline: "I have always dreamed of saying in a song to the Blessed Virgin everything I think about her." Sr. Marie of the Sacred Heart anticipated this yearning, and asked her to write something on the Blessed Virgin, which she did in the month of May, 1897. Thérèse, as with all her writing, went to the Gospel for inspiration. There she found Mary as she truly is — with all the virtues of a hidden, heroic life of love and suffering, which we all can strive to imitate. Her poem, *Why I love You, O Mary!* was her last and most moving poem. One line of this twenty five stanza poem summarizes well her reason for loving Mary so passionately, "To love is to give everything. It's to give oneself [as Mary did]."

One of her former novices, Sister Marie of the Trinity, explains Thérèse's *modus operandi*: "Her ignorance [of poetic rules] was voluntary. When I entered Carmel in June 1894, I had brought a treatise on versification. She glanced at it and gave it back to me right away, and said: 'I prefer not to know all those rules. My poems are spurts from my heart, inspirations. I wouldn't know how to tie myself down to toil in spirit, to study. At this price, I would prefer to renounce writing poetry.'

In most cases Thérèse's poems were meant to be sung especially during recreation periods. She simply replaced existing lyrics with her own words. She chose the music herself from familiar childhood melodies, arias from well-known operas, and from contemporary songs. Thérèse's melodious harmonies resound throughout her poems with their exuberant praise of the divine and their profound and passionate expressions of her love.

She wrote requested poems for particular occasions such as feast days, birthdays, holidays and anniversaries. Not all the poems were for others. Some were expressions of her own spiritual inspirations and for personal reflection. The poems of Thérèse have been variably classified by critics as brilliant, mediocre or poor. The story behind the composition of her first poem that was requested by Sister Teresa of St. Augustine (a nun toward whom Thérèse had a natural antipathy): "One day I [Sister Teresa of St. Augustine] asked her to write a canticle on our favorite subject, the Holy Infancy of Jesus. 'That's impossible,' she replied, I don't know anything about poetry.' I answered, 'What does that matter? We're not going to send it to the *Academie française*. This is just to make me happy and so satisfy a desire of my soul.' Sister Thérèse replied, 'I still hesitate because I don't know if this is God's will.' I said then, 'Oh! I'll give you some advice about that. Before you start to write, ask Our Lord: 'My God, if this is not your will, I ask you for the grace not to be able to succeed at it. But if this is for your glory, help me.' I believe that after that you will have nothing to worry about.' She followed my advice and that is how she wrote her first poem."

Thérèse's entire life was a song of praise to the Lord, as she even acknowledged in the very beginning of her autobiography: "I shall begin to sing what I must sing eternally: 'The Mercies of the Lord.'" At a later date, we read a statement recalling one of her poems, *To scatter flowers*: "While I am strewing my flowers [at the cross in the cloister courtyard] 'I shall sing, . . . I shall sing even when I must gather flowers in the midst of thorns, and my song will be all the more melodious in proportion to the length and sharpness of the thorns."

During the last eighteen months of her life when she experienced such desolation and temptations against faith that she was afraid to relate it in detail, she wrote in her *Story of a Soul*, "If you are judging according to the sentiments I express in my little poems composed this year, I must appear to you as a soul filled with consolations and one for whom the veil of faith is almost torn aside; . . .When I sing of the happiness of heaven and of the eternal possession of God, I feel no joy in this, for I sing simply what I want to believe." The bitter trial of faith continued from Easter 1896 until her death in September 1897, thereby placing nearly the last half of all her poems within the time frame of this tormented phase of her spiritual journey.

In conclusion, Thérèse reveals lyrically her deep mystical concepts and values in metaphorical, poetic language that prose is incapable of conveying whether it be childhood reminiscences, liturgical celebrations, adulation of the saints or the Blessed Virgin, or meditation on her love of Jesus. By reading *Story of a Soul* first and then her poems one is struck by the resemblance between the two, how the poems expound upon the same subjects that occupied her daily thoughts and actions that she records so tellingly in her autobiography. They are a perfect mirror of her beliefs expressed in a more intense, concentrated, and symbolic style. Now with all her poems available in a superb English translations they may be read and contemplated by every devotee of the Little Saint of Lisieux.

A floral design on the floor of the chapter room where Thérèse prostrated herself when making her religious profession.

Part VII

1. The Spiritual Father of Thérèse: St. John of the Cross

Fr. J. Carmel O'Shea, D.D.

2. Act of Oblation to the Merciful Love of God

St. Thérèse of the Child Jesus and Holy Face

3. Kolbe's Total Consecration — In Respect to Thérèse's Oblation to God's Merciful Love

Fr. Thomas M. Huff, F.I.

4. St. Thérèse — Saint of the Eucharist

Fr. Stéphane Jos. Piat, O.F.M.

The Spiritual Father of Thérèse: St. John of the Cross

By Fr. J. Carmel O'Shea, D.D.

No one who has read *Story of a Soul* can doubt that the writings of St. John of the Cross played an important part in the spiritual life of St. Therese of the Child Jesus. This is not to be wondered at, for St. John of the Cross wrote *ex professo* for the nuns of the Reform, and his works, like those of St. Teresa of Avila herself have a particular authority for all Carmelites desirous of ascending the holy mountain of contemplation and attaining to divine union.

What might surprise us, however, is that the little saint of Lisieux should have so completely and profoundly grasped the teaching of her spiritual father; for the writings of St. John of the Cross, dealing as they do with "the deep things of God," do not make easy reading. The author of the *Ascent*, the *Dark Night* and the *Canticle* speaks the same language as she.

For her there is no obscurity, no difficulty; she has passed his way; she knows it well. Her soul has lived and loved as St. John of the Cross had lived and loved, and therefore his writings are for her clear and authoritative, pointing out the path to the summit of perfection and Divine Love.

Although her references to these writings are not numerous—not more than eight in *Story of a Soul* and five in her letters to her sister Céline, yet she has herself testified to the debt she owed to the works of the Mystic Doctor in words which have been quoted frequently, but the full implication of which has not, perhaps, been so often realized. In *Story of a Soul* we read: "The works of St. John of the Cross have been such a source of light to me. Between the ages of sixteen and eighteen I read no one else. Later on, spiritual writers always left me cold, and still do."

In his pages she found both an analysis and a synthesis of everything that she had already experienced or was likely to experience on her journey to the heights of Carmel. With keen and eager intellect and heart aglow with love she applied his words to her own soul, and lo, the shadows fell apart and she saw clearly set out before her the path she was to follow to the heights of Love. She sees how Jesus drew her specially to Himself emptying her heart of every desire for creatures by means of a spiritual bond which had grown up between herself and her sister Céline, when she was about fourteen years of age. "Since Christmas I had taken Céline completely into my confidence, and Jesus, who wanted us to go forward side by side, bound our hearts together with ties far stronger than those of blood, and made us sisters in spirit too, so that the words of St. John of the Cross came true for us:

> 'Lightly the maidens tread the way
> Thy footsteps passed, Beloved One;
> The touch of the spark
> And the spicèd wine
> Bring to their lips the fragrant words
> Of love divine.'

"Our hearts were certainly light as we followed in His footsteps, the sparks which He scattered in our souls, the spiced wine He offered us to drink made us oblivious of everything on earth, and aspirations full of love sprang to our lips."

As in these earliest spiritual experiences, so too in the matter of her vocation, Thérèse found accurately expressed in the beautiful imagery of St. John of the Cross the over-powering love that burned within her heart, and lit with gladdening rays the dark and lowering path of contradictions and refusals along which she had to travel before she could come into the Land of Carmel and give herself entirely to her Beloved who there awaited her:

> "I had no guide, no light
> Save that which burned within my heart,
> And yet this light did guide my way,
> More surely than the noonday sun
> Unto the place where waited One
> Who knew me well."

St. John of the Cross, commenting on these words, says: "It is well to understand that the soul which utters them is now in a state of perfection, which is the union of love with God, having already passed through severe trials and straits by means of spiritual exercise in the narrow way of eternal life whereof Our Saviour speaks in the Gospel, along which the soul ordinarily passes in order to reach this high and happy union with

God." St. Thérèse's own remarks on this stanza confirm what the great Doctor has written. "This place was Carmel, but before I could *'sit down under His shadow whom I desired,'* I had to go through many tribulations. Yet the divine call was always so urgent, that even if it had meant going through fire, I would have cast myself in to follow Him."

The years following her profession saw the fire of divine love fed and nourished with suffering of soul and body grow ever more intense within her heart. It purged of all its human regret the distressing illness and death of her dear father. Because it was so fruitful of love, she could even refer to the time of his sickness as "our great treasure"; for she had come to that stage where, in the words of St. John of the Cross, "the soul is filled with wondrous desires to work and suffer for the Divine Spouse," and to suffer and to love was now her only joy.

Her vocation had now reached its full flowering. Jesus Himself had called to her and drawn her to Himself in religion; and now she had given her heart and all her affections entirely to Him. As before, in describing the preparation of her soul and her vocation to Carmel, so now too the words of her spiritual father, St. John of the Cross, burst spontaneously from her lips to express the completeness of her preoccupation with love. She writes: "I am guided by self-abandonment alone, and need no other compass, no longer knowing how to ask for anything with eagerness except that God may do His will completely in my soul."

She says that she is occupied no longer in those things which concern herself, but in those which pertain to the service of her Spouse, and that for this reason she no longer goes about seeking her own gain, nor pursues her own tastes, nor busies herself in other things, and in intercourse which has naught to do with God and is alien to Him. And that even with God Himself she has no other style or manner of intercourse save the exercise of love. But the soul thus described by St. John of the Cross is one who has attained to union with God. "Happy life and happy estate and happy the soul which arrives thereat," he writes, "where all is now substance of love to it, and joy and delight of betrothal!" And he concludes his exposition thus: "The soul in this estate of the spiritual betrothal walks habitually in the union of the love of God, which is the common and habitual presence of the loving will of God." St. Thérèse with childlike simplicity saw that these words mirrored her soul, and so with the same childlike simplicity and humility she made them her own.

We find, then, in the chapter on fraternal charity, the following reference to St. John of the Cross: "I must admit that I am far from doing what I know I ought to do, but the very desire to do so brings me peace. If I happen to fall into some fault against charity I get up again at once; for some months now I have not even had to struggle. I can say with St. John of the Cross 'my house is entirely at peace' and I attribute this peace to a certain victory I gained."

There is little need to describe that victory; readers of *The Story of a Soul* will readily recall it, nor is it necessary for the purpose of our study. What is necessary is that we should grasp the significance of the words: "My house is entirely at peace," and to do this we must turn once more for an explanation to the writings of St. John of the Cross. This verse is the most characteristic of his work. It occurs twice in the poem *The Dark Night of the Soul* wherein he describes the successive purgations or purifications of the soul in its journey towards union with God. The author tells us that the first purification is that of our sensual nature. The fruits of this "Dark Night of the Senses," as it is called, are four-fold, namely delight of peace, habitual remembrance and thoughts of God, cleanliness and purity of soul, and the practice of the virtues.

The soul thus purged of affections and desires of the senses obtains wonderful liberty of spirit and "is wondrously delivered from the hands of its three enemies, the devil, the world and the flesh; for its pleasure and delight of sense being quenched with respect to all things, neither the devil nor the world nor sensuality has any arms or strength wherewith to make war upon the spirit." Thus delivered, the soul can say with truth regarding the life of the senses, "My house is entirely at peace." St. Thérèse had long attained to this peace. Even as a child she had passed through this purgation, emptying her soul of every desire of sense.

But there comes now to specially chosen souls a second and more terrible "night" — the "Dark night of the Soul." Those whom God calls to highest union must for the most part pass through this union. The whole of the second part of the exposition of the poem *The Dark Night* deals with this dark night of the soul, and in it St. John of the Cross reaches the most sublime heights of all his mystical writings. The soul, having at length, through God's mercy, emerged triumphant from this night, again repeats the words: "My house is entirely at peace," on which St. John comments: "This is as much as to say: The higher portion of my soul being like the lower part also, at rest with respect to its desires and faculties, I went forth to the Divine Union of the love of God."

Thus we can affirm that the words are quoted and used by St. Thérèse of the Child Jesus truly, and in the fullest sense as expounded by the holy Doctor of Carmel; for when she wrote them, she had indeed attained to that deep and tranquil interior peace and to the Divine Union which follows. St. John tells us that when the two houses of the soul have become tranquilized, the Divine Wisdom immediately unites itself with the soul by making a new bond of loving possession. Very significant, then, is the use of these words by St. Thérèse of the Child Jesus, for they show her as having attained to the complete conquest of self and to the possession of that interior peace which ever marks the soul in union of love with God.

This shows us how completely she had made the teaching of St. John of the Cross her own; for only one who had thus mastered that teaching could use his words with such unerring propriety. The mastery indicated here is that of the soul which has "lived" that teaching, whose life is an exposition of what is there set down.

Her final words from her father in Carmel need an explanation, for both are rules of love which she had ever made her own: "Love is repaid by love alone," a phrase which she adopted as her motto; and "The least act of pure love is of more value to her (the Church) than all other works together." It was fitting that these words of pure gold should be her last offering to us from that rich mine of spiritual treasure of which she was so fully possessed.

From St. John of the Cross she finds the spiritual explanation: *"All good things have come to me since I no longer seek them for myself"* This pithy sentence enshrines one of the fundamental maxims of the great Carmelite Doctor, summed up especially in the instructions on how we may attain to the All, appended to his map of the Mount of Perfection. St. Thérèse shows us clearly how it reveals itself in, and may be applied to, the ordinary everyday affairs of community life. She applies it, in a word, to her Little Way, and in doing so, throws much clear and helpful light on the manner in which we can use the Little Way in our own lives.

By tracing the spiritual growth and progress of St. Thérèse of the Child Jesus along the purest and most typical path of perfection as laid down by St. John of the Cross, we come to the obvious conclusion that her Little Way of Spiritual Childhood is the highest and purest path to spiritual perfection, since all her progress to God was made along it. This, to my mind, is an unanswerable argument for all those who scorn the Little Way and see in it only childishness, despite the fact that it has been acclaimed by the Supreme Pontiffs. It is consoling, too, to remember that as the very essence of the Little Way is that it lies within the reach of very ordinary souls, even the highest perfection of love of God can be attained by all who earnestly strive to follow this path.

— A condesation of the article "St. Thérèse and St. John of the Cross," reprinted with permission from *Sicut Parvuli.*

She Smiled Upon Her Child

While the novena of Masses was still being said, [at our Lady of Victories] Marie went out into the garden, one Sunday morning, . . . After a few minutes I began to call for Marie, in a voice hardly above a whisper: 'Mamma! Mamma!'. . . It went on and on; my cries became louder; and in the end Marie came back. I was quite conscious of her entering the room, but I couldn't recognize with any certainty who it was, so I went on calling. . . . When she found she couldn't convince me that she was really there, she knelt down beside my bed, with Léonie and Céline, turned towards our Lady's statue and prayed for me like a mother praying for her child's life. And her prayer, Marie's prayer, was granted.

There was no help, it seemed, for poor Thérèse on earth; so I, too, had turned towards the statue, and all my heart went out into a prayer that my Mother in Heaven would have pity on me. All at once, she let me see her in her beauty, a beauty that surpassed all my experience, her face wore such a look of kindness and of pity as I can't describe; but what pierced me to the heart was her smile, 'that entrancing smile of the Blessed Virgin's.' With that, all my distress came to an end; two big tears started up from my eyes, and ran softly down my cheeks; but they were tears of joy, unadulterated joy.

And I said to myself: 'To think that the Blessed Virgin should have smiled down at me! Oh, I'm so happy! . . . I could see Marie looking at me tenderly, profoundly moved and yet not quite certain about the grace our Lady had granted me. Or rather, granted her; it was to her pathetic prayers that I owed this privilege of a smile from the Queen of Heaven herself. The moment she saw my eyes fixed on the statue, she thought: 'Thérèse has recovered!' And she was right; the faded flower had come to life again, . . . and grew so strong that it could unfold itself five years later, on the rich mountain soil of Carmel.

Excepted from the translation of Msgr. Ronald Knox's, *Story of a Soul.*

ACT OF OBLATION TO THE MERCIFUL LOVE OF GOD

J.M.J.T.

9th June 1895

Offering of myself as a Victim of Holocaust to God's Merciful Love

O My God! Most Blessed Trinity, I desire to Love You and make You Loved, to work for the glory of Holy Church by saving souls on earth and liberating those suffering in purgatory. I desire to accomplish Your will perfectly and to reach the degree of glory You have prepared for me in Your Kingdom. I desire, in a word, to be a saint, but I feel my helplessness and I beg You, O my God! to be Yourself my Sanctity!

I offer You, too, all the merits of the saints (in heaven and on earth), their acts of Love, and those of the holy angels. Finally, I offer You, O Blessed Trinity! the Love and merits of the Blessed Virgin, my dear Mother. It is to her I abandon my offering, begging her to present it to You. Her Divine Son, my Beloved Spouse, told us in the days of His mortal life: "Whatsoever you ask the Father in my name he will give it to you!" I am certain, then, that You will grant my desires; I know, O my God! that the more You want to give, the more You make us desire. I feel in my heart immense desires and it is with confidence I ask You to come and take possession of my soul. Ah! I cannot receive Holy Communion as often as I desire, but, Lord, are You not all-powerful? Remain in me as in a tabernacle and never separate Yourself from Your little victim.

I want to console You for the ingratitude of the wicked, and I beg of You to take away my freedom to displease You. If through weakness I sometimes fall, may Your Divine Glance cleanse my soul immediately, consuming all my imperfections like the fire that transforms everything into itself.

I thank You, O my God! for all the graces You have granted me, especially the grace of making me pass through the crucible of suffering. It is with joy I shall contemplate You on the Last Day carrying the scepter of Your Cross. Since You deigned to give me a share in this very precious Cross, I hope in heaven to resemble You and to see shining in my glorified body the sacred stigmata of Your Passion.

After earth's Exile, I hope to go and enjoy You in the Fatherland, but I do not want to lay up merits for heaven. I want to work for Your Love alone with the one purpose of pleasing You, consoling Your Sacred Heart, and saving souls who will love You eternally.

Wounded by Fire of Love

The act of Oblation opened up to St. Thérèse in her own words, "Oceans of graces, which inundated my soul immediately after this donation of myself on June 9, 1895. Just a few days later, while in the choir making the Way of the Cross, ... I felt myself suddenly wounded by a dart of fire so ardent that I thought I should die. I know not how to describe that transport: there is no comparison which would make the vehemence of that flame understood. It seemed as though an invisible force plunged me wholly into fire. Oh, that fire! What sweetness! One minute, one second more, and my soul must have been set free. . ."

In the evening of this life, I shall appear before You with empty hands, for I do not ask You, Lord, to count my works. All our justice is stained in Your eyes. I wish, then, to be clothed in Your own Justice and to receive from Your Love the eternal possession of Yourself. I want no other Throne, no other Crown but You, my Beloved!

Time is nothing in Your eyes, and a single day is like a thousand years. You can, then, in one instant, prepare me to appear before You.

In order to live in one single act of perfect Love, I offer Myself as a Victim of Holocaust to Your Merciful Love, asking You to consume me incessantly, allowing the waves of infinite tenderness shut up within You to overflow into my soul, and that thus I may become a martyr of Your Love, O my God! May this martyrdom, after having prepared me to appear before You, finally cause me to die and may my soul take its flight without any delay into the eternal embrace of Your Merciful Love. I want, O my Beloved at each beat of my heart to renew this offering to You an infinite number of times, until the shadows having disappeared I may be able to tell You of my Love in an *Eternal Face to Face!*

Marie Françoise Thérèse of the Child Jesus and the Holy Face, unworthy Carmelite religious.

Kolbe's Total Consecration
and Thérèse's Oblation to
God's Merciful Love

By Father Thomas Mary Huff, F.I.

Two years before her death, St. Thérèse wrote what is called her Act of Oblation to God's Merciful Love. It is a summary of her whole plan of life. This brief document expressed her ardent desire to be a victim or holocaust of love offered in atonement to God for mankind's rejecting His merciful love. She offered this oblation through the mediation of the Blessed Virgin, for the salvation of souls. The same aspiration can be seen throughout the writings of St. Maximilian Mary Kolbe, and had been succinctly expressed by him on October 16, 1917, when he made his act of total consecration to the Immaculate. This chapter intends to highlight the likeness of their spiritualities, in the hope that it may benefit those who are seeking a simple, easy and sure way to holiness. — *The Author of this Chapter*

On January 14, 1930, Saint Maximilian Mary Kolbe journeyed from Poland to Rome for the purpose of obtaining permission from his Father General to begin a new mission in Japan. When asked by the Father General if he had any financial support for this new project and if he knew the Japanese language, he answered in the negative to both. Surprisingly, the Father General did give him the necessary permission. Perhaps it was St. Maximilian's aura of total confidence that such a mission would succeed, that won over the somewhat skeptical Father General. It was certainly not in himself that St. Maximilian placed his confidence. In fact, before his return to Poland he went to Lourdes to place his entire mission endeavor in the hands of the Immaculate. On his way to the Orient he stopped over at Lisieux to beg Saint Thérèse, as did other missionaries at that time, to assist him in his missionary efforts.

This double confidence on the part of St. Maximilian in both the Immaculate Virgin Mary and St. Thérèse is no coincidence. St. Thérèse was known not only for her enthusiastic regard for the Church's missionary activity, but more importantly for her desire to be an instrument totally in the hands of God through Mary's mediation. No doubt this aspiration was identical to St. Maximilian's. Early in 1912, as a_young Franciscan student, he took quite an interest in the famous autobiography, *Story of a Soul*. He even made an agreement with the saintly Carmelite nun, who at that time had not yet been beatified: "If you obtain for me the grace of perseverance in the Order, and the attainment of priesthood, I will pray for your beatification and canonization." St. Maximilian persevered and was ordained, and Thérèse was beatified and canonized. The agreement was kept!

The profound Marian spirituality of these two Saints began at an early age. Both had extraordinary experiences involving the Blessed Virgin which would have lasting effects on their whole life. During the year of 1882, at the age of nine, St. Thérèse had succumbed to a strange and almost deadly illness, affecting both physical and mental health. Her father realizing the seriousness of her condition had a novena of Masses offered in honor of Our Lady of Victory. Shortly after this St. Thérèse writes:

> Finding no help on earth, poor little Thérèse had also (her sisters were storming heaven too) turned towards the Mother of God, and prayed with all her heart that she take pity on her. All of a sudden the Blessed Virgin appeared *beautiful* to me, so *beautiful* that never had I seen anything so attractive; her face was suffused with an ineffable benevolence and tenderness, but what penetrated to the very depths of my soul was the *"ravishing smile of the Blessed Virgin."* At that instant, all my pain disappeared, and two large tears glistened on my eyelashes, and flowed down my cheeks silently,...

It was this healing experience of St. Thérèse that had a profound effect on her striving for holiness, eventually stripping away every encumbrance in the way of her divine Spouse. At the age of ten, Saint Maximilian also had a similarly intimate encounter with the Immaculate Virgin. He had exasperated his mother one day and after being chided he went to a nearby church to ask the Blessed Mother what would become of him. He tells us:

> One day when I was praying in church before the picture of Mary Immaculate, she suddenly became alive and showed me two crowns. One was white, the other red. The first symbolized purity, the second martyrdom. She asked me which I would choose. I chose both.

The Blessed Virgin had chosen these two Saints for our times for a very special mission — a mission which would require great sacrifice and heroism. Eventually, they both consecrated themselves to the Blessed Virgin Mary. Saint Thérèse, eleven years old at the time, recounts this important event in her life:

As a boy St. Maximilian was offered the crowns of martyrdom and purity. He chose both, vowing chastity and dying in the cruel concentration camp of Auschwitz. The symbolic painting was used at his canonization ceremony in 1982.

In the afternoon, it was I who made the Act of Consecration to the Blessed Virgin... I put all my heart into *speaking* to her, into consecrating myself to her as a child throwing herself into the arms of its mother, asking her to watch over her. It seems to me the Blessed Virgin must have looked upon her little flower and *smiled* at her, for wasn't it she who cured her with a *visible smile*? Has she not placed in the heart of her little flower her Jesus, the Flower of the Fields and the Lily of the valley.

This consecration was no passing devotion, she truly desired to belong totally to Mary as her child. Two years later she showed her love for the Blessed Mother in a way that demanded sacrifice on the part of this extremely sensitive child. As she was no longer a student at the Benedictine Abbey school, she would have to prove her love for Mary to the school mistress by sitting alone in the school chapel for two afternoons a week for about a year. As she tells us:

Thinking that all my sisters had been "children of Mary," I feared I would be less a child of my heavenly Mother than they were. I went very humbly (in spite of what it cost me) to ask permission to be received into the Association . . . . Ah! it was really for the Blessed Virgin alone that I was coming to the Abbey. Sometimes I felt *alone*, very much *alone*.

The twenty-three year-old Friar Maximilian, made his total consecration to the Immaculate Virgin with six other friars in the Franciscan seminary chapel in Rome. It was there that he established the international movement, the *Militia Immaculatae*. Five years later while writing to another friar he explains the importance of the act of consecration in relation to the *Militia Immaculatae*: "Hence, strictly speaking, it is our consecration to our Lady Immaculate (an interior act) according to the spirit of the M.I., as one who is unconditionally and totally her instrument in life, death and eternity, as one who is her property, that constitutes the essence of the M.I."

Some people today might find consecration to Mary or the thought of becoming her child a throw back to less "enlightened times," even unnecessary. Yet St. Maximilian advises all who are striving for holiness to become a child of Mary in a most compelling manner. He suggests following the example of God Himself: "Let us turn our gaze towards Jesus, our most perfect Model. He who is God, supreme Holiness, gives Himself to the Immaculate without reserve and becomes her Son. He chose her to guide Him, as she pleased, for thirty years of His earthly life. Do we perhaps need a more encouraging example? . . . Let us follow Jesus' lead."

At the very center of their spirituality both St. Thérèse and St. Maximilian desired to be perfectly conformed to the will of God, purely out of love. In her Act of Oblation or Offering to God's Merciful Love, St. Thérèse begins with a recognition of God's will and a desire to become a saint through perfect union with His will: "O my God! Most Blessed Trinity . . . I desire to accomplish Your will perfectly and to reach the degree of glory You have prepared for me in Your Kingdom. I desire, in a word, to be a saint." St. Maximilian likewise expresses the same thought writing, "Our soul's degree of perfection depends on the union of our will with that of God. The greater the perfection, the closer the union." However, both understood that such an intimate and consummate union between themselves and God was achieved most perfectly through the mediation of Mary Immaculate.

The consecration to Mary, which they had made earlier in their lives, had permeated their whole being and was to find expression in like words and actions. St. Thérèse in her act of oblation succinctly states: "Finally, I offer You, O *Blessed Trinity*! the love and merits of **the Blessed Virgin**, *my dear Mother*. **It is to her I abandon my offering, begging her to present it to You**" (emphasis added). Likewise, St. Maximilian in his "act of consecration" addresses his heavenly Mother: ". . . **my most loving Mother** . . . I cast myself at your feet, and humbly beseech **you to accept me wholly and entirely, as your property and posses-sion** . . . so that in your immaculate and merciful hands I may become a useful instrument. . . **to extend** . . . **as far as possible, the marvelous reign of the Sacred Heart of Jesus**" (emphasis added). St. Maximilian explains his understanding of Mary's mediation more profoundly when he wrote: "The more one belongs to the Immaculate, the more freely and openly can he draw near to the wounds of our Savior, to the Holy Eucharist, to the Sacred Heart of Jesus, to God our Father. Further, I shall tell him that it is not at all necessary that the thought of the Immaculate should occupy his mind at every particular moment; for the essence of our union with her does not consist in thought, memory or sentiment, but in our will."

When St. Thérèse was experiencing the "Dark night of the soul" and God seemed hidden from her, she was asked by Mother Agnes of Jesus (her sister Pauline), if the Blessed Virgin was also hidden from her. The Saint responded:

No, the Blessed Virgin is never hidden from me. And when I can no longer see the good God, she takes care of all my dealings with Him. I

St. Thérèse in the role of St. Joan of Arc in the play that she wrote and performed for the sisters in the Carmel at Lisieux in 1894. She admired immensely the great national heroine, who dying at 19 whispered the sweet name of Jesus.

commission her especially to tell Him to have no fear of sending me trials. The Blessed Virgin really carried out my messages well; . . . I'll tell her very often: "Tell Him never to put Himself out on my account." He has heard this, and this is exactly what He's doing. I no longer understand anything about my sickness. Here I am getting better! However, I abandon myself to Him and I'm happy just the same. What would become of me if I did not nourish the hope of soon dying? What disappointments! But I don't have a single one, because I am totally content with what God does; I desire only His will.

It certainly is true that St. Thérèse had great devotion to the saints, especially Joan of Arc, Theophane Venard, John of the Cross and Teresa of Avila. Nonetheless, her offering to God was made through the mediation of the Virgin Mary. In a conversation to Sister Marie of the Sacred Heart (her eldest sister Marie) we come to understand why:

"When we address ourselves to the saints, they make us wait a little, and we feel that they have to go and present their request; but whenever I ask a favor from the Blessed Virgin, I receive immediate help. . . Haven't you ever noticed this? Try it yourself, and you'll see." St. Maximilian understood very well what St. Thérèse was saying. And he clarifies precisely how the Immaculate is able to be so effective in her mediation with God: "The soul offers the Immaculate its own acts of love not as one hands over an object to any ordinary go-between, but as her very own, giving her full and exclusive right to them. It understands that the Immaculate will offer to Jesus these acts as if they were really her own. This means that she will offer them to Jesus without any defect, immaculate, and Jesus will then offer them to the Father."

The humble and yet profound spirituality of these two Saints, enabled them to recognize their own limitations both in their desires and in their works, as they tried to express their love of God. Because their humility allowed them to see themselves as small and dependent children before God, they saw the need to be all the more dependent on Mary's help. These two Saints fully realized that with Mary's help their own desires and works would be more perfectly purified of all self-love and imperfections. St. Thérèse writes:

I have asked this from the Blessed Virgin. I didn't ask God because I want Him to do as He pleases. Asking the Blessed Virgin for something is not the same as asking God. She really knows what is to be done about my little desires, whether or not she must speak about them to God. So it's up to her to see that God is not forced to answer me, to allow Him to do everything as He pleases.

The Saint from Lisieux also reveals her total dependence upon Mary in her Autobiography: "The Blessed Virgin . . . never fails to protect me as soon as I invoke her. If some disturbance overtakes me, some embarrassment, I turn very quickly to her and as the most tender of Mothers she always takes care of my interests." And even her great desire to be a Carmelite missionary is conditioned on the disposition of her heavenly Mother: ". . . your [Mother Gonzague] apostolic desire finds a faithful echo in my own soul, as you know; but let me confide why I desired and still desire **if the Blessed Virgin cures me** (added emphasis), to leave the delightful oasis of the Carmel here. . ."

St. Maximilian too discloses his total dependence on Mary to perfect all his plans and works; in one of his letters we read:

> Since we belong entirely to the Immaculate, let us do all within our power to convert and sanctify souls. It is the Immaculate herself who works through our mediation. . . . those acts become more perfect because they become the possession of the Immaculate. She will carry them out in our stead much better than we ourselves could. . . . We belong to her, to the Immaculate. . . . And Jesus, considering us her property and, as it were, a part of his beloved Mother, loves her in us and through us. What a lovely mystery!

This mystery of belonging totally to Mary and depending on her mediation for the fruitfulness of all their desires and works, is really the key to the success of these two Saints, in their quest for holiness and perfect union with the Blessed Trinity. So complete was their dependency and confidence in Mary's maternal mediation, that even when their prayers did not bring about the expected results, they did not grow discouraged or despondent. St. Thérèse writes: "When we pray to the Blessed Virgin and she doesn't answer, that's a sign she doesn't want to. Then its better to leave her alone and not torment ourselves." St. Maximilian also concludes: "If it is our Mom's [Mary's] thing, then difficulties will only strengthen it; but if not, then let it fail like anything else. . . . let her do as she pleases. Let's be occupied, but not preoccupied."

Indeed, both Saints had clearly understood that holiness consists solely in uniting one's will to the will of God, and that such an aim is most perfectly achieved, by God's design, only through the mediation of the Blessed Virgin. Without doubt, their perceptive understanding and intense desire for perfect union with God's will came about precisely because of their continued growth in their trust in and dependency upon Mary's mediation.

Recently, Pope John Paul II has declared St. Thérèse a Doctor of the Church. Perhaps some day Saint Maximilian too may be raised to such a dignity. Their spirituality is extremely similar and simple, and so necessary in our days of skepticism and sophistication. People are yearning for meaning in their lives, they are looking for ways and means to be loved and express love, for which they were created. Tragically, many are locked into the deceptions and lies of materialism, satanism, hedonism and atheism. Love which they crave and desire to share is lost on superficial things or turned into lust and hatred, something twisted and inverted.

It is only under the guidance and protection of a loving Mother that we can once again find our way to true love in the bosom of the Blessed Trinity. This was the secret of the *Little Way* espoused by both St. Thérèse and St. Maximilian. A year before his heroic death in Auschwitz, St. Maximilian speaking to God wrote:

> You commanded us to become like little children, if we wish to enter the kingdom of Heaven. . . . You know well enough that a child needs a mother; for You Yourself have established that law of love. Therefore, in your goodness and mercy You created a mother for us, the personification of your goodness and your infinite love; and from the Cross on Golgotha you offered her to us, and us to her. Further, You have ordained, O God, who loves us, that she should be the all-powerful dispenser and Mediatrix of all graces. You do not refuse her anything; and in her turn she is not able to refuse anything to anyone. . . . Who will fail to reach paradise? Probably only a fool, a stubborn hater of himself, who consciously and willingly does not want to be saved . . . and actually runs away from the best of mothers, despising her mediation.

The best way to honor the Saints is by imitation. Therefore, let us follow the lead of these two spiritual giants and embrace Mary as our good Mother. And let us above all, imitate our Divine Savior who chose her to be His Mother and teacher as well as ours. Let us consecrate our lives to Mary, totally and entirely so that she may form us, after the example of St. Thérèse, into victims of God's Merciful Love. Thérèse promised to rise up a whole army of victim souls to God's Merciful Love, which is assured if we give ourselves totally, without reserve to His infinite love and mercy through the Immaculate Heart of Mary.

"On the day of my first Communion we were no longer two: Thérèse had disappeared as a drop of water lost in the ocean. Only Jesus remained. He was the Master, the king. Had not Thérèse asked Him to take away her freedom? The thought of being free frightened her. She felt so weak that she wanted to become one with the strength of God."
—St. Thérèse, *Story of a Soul*

Saint of the Eucharist

Fr. Stéphane Jos. Piat, O.F.M.

The freezing wind of Jansenism which kept the faithful away from the Holy Table, replacing the image of the All-Merciful God by that of a God to be feared above all, never penetrated the household of Monsieur and Madame Martin. Every morning these valiant Christians assisted at the 5:30 Mass; and they went to Communion as frequently as they were allowed at that time. For the father especially, visits to the Blessed Sacrament, the Holy Hour, nocturnal adoration were the mainspring of his spiritual life and the home life of his family. Thérèse grew up in that environment. In her daily walks, usually with her father, she paid a visit to one Tabernacle or another in the town. As a half-boarder at school she daily spent, at 1:30, a quarter of an hour of her free time in company with Jesus in the tabernacle. Her teachers and companions have testified that her attitude during the divine services was like that of a contemplative soul.

She felt it keenly that she could not approach the Holy Eucharist more easily. Her sister Marie explained how young children were admitted to Holy Communion during the first centuries in the Church. "And why," she exclaimed, "is it not like that now?" One Christmas night — she was only six or seven at the time — she wanted to steal up, unnoticed, and receive Holy Communion between her father and Marie. According to diocesan regulations, she could not receive her First Communion before the age of eleven. But, as she was born on January 2 she would lose a whole year. During a Sunday walk with her sisters, they happened to see the bishop, and she wanted to go to him and ask a dispensation from that year. At least she would make up for the delay by the fervour of her preparation for her First Communion. Using a method specially arranged and written out for her by her sister Pauline, she applied herself to the preparation daily during two months and a half, and offered 818 little acts of sacrifice, with 2,773 aspirations of love.

Her First Communion was a turning point in her life. She was lost in Jesus. "It was no longer a meeting [of friends], it was a fusion of hearts" (see article on Mystical Simplicity, page 7). That was May 8, 1884; the same dream-ecstasy was renewed on May 22, at her second Communion.

If she had listened only to her heart, she would have gone to the Communion rail every morning. But, child of obedience, she did not seek to follow her own initiative. Her confessor, treating her as a privileged child, permitted her four or five communions a week. "This permission," she wrote, "coming straight from Our Lord, filled me with joy. In those days I did not dare speak of my intimate feelings; but now I am quite sure one should mention to one's confessor the desire to receive Our Lord. It is not to remain alone in a golden ciborium that He comes down every day from heaven, but to find another heaven infinitely dearer to Him: the heaven of our soul, created in His image, the living temple of the adorable Trinity."

In the Carmel there was a different trial. Regulations in force at that time conferred on the superiors the right of admitting the religious to the Holy Table. Mother Mary Gonzague adhered to the strict interpretation. Thérèse was grieved to find herself admitted only once a week. She addressed a special prayer to St. Joseph that he might obtain a more lenient interpretation. She may be said to have obtained a first victory. By a Rescript from the Holy See, December 17, 1890, Leo XIII transferred

As a child, throwing rose petals before the Blessed Sacrament. Nothing gave her more pleasure than when they touched the monstrance. Right: As sacristan in the convent of Lisieux. It was a source of great joy to be privileged to handle the Sacred Vessels in which Jesus would become present.

to the confessor-chaplains of religious communities the right of prescribing the frequency of Holy Communion.

In one of her poems, "My Desires Before the Tabernacle," she expressed her longing to remain ever close to the Divine Prisoner. The tabernacle key, the sanctuary lamp, the altar-stone, the corporal and paten, the chalice, and the sacramental species are images on which she fixes her fervent imagination. She expressed poetically her heart's desire:

> Thy Spouse am I. Thy chosen one,
> My Well-beloved; Come, dwell in me.
> Oh come! Thy beauty wins my heart.
> Deign to transform me into Thee.

Thérèse's deep spirit of faith inspired her with great reverence for priests because of their sacerdotal dignity, a dignity which could never be too highly esteemed. Though she often expressed a certain regret at her own exclusion from the priesthood, her office of sacristan offered her consoling compensations. She would look at her face mirrored within the chalice; she tenderly prepared the Mass vestments.

She would not brook the suggestion that it would be advisable, on account of her illness, to omit one of her Communions, granted to her all too rarely by the house rule. Mother Gonzague once asked her to take some medicine which would break her Eucharistic fast, but Thérèse, by her tears, begged to be allowed to go to Communion first. During the last five weeks of her life, when physical suffering was consuming her strength, and moral anguish was entirely clouding her soul, her greatest affliction was that she could not receive Holy Communion. It is true, she had a remedy for everything. Her "soul of desires" linked her hope to the infinite Goodness of God. In her "Act of Oblation," she dared to say: "I cannot receive Holy Communion as often as I desire, but, dear Lord, are You not omnipotent?. . . Remain within me as in the Tabernacle."

She had a prophetic intuition that after her death access to the Tabernacle would be made much easier. Speaking of a priest, an apostle of frequent Communion, she said to one of her sisters: "Perhaps the time will come when we shall have Abbé Hodierne as our Chaplain, and then he will give us daily Holy Communion." The remark was regarded as incredible. Yet, Abbé Hodierne became Chaplain of the Carmel and his first instruction was "Come, and eat this Bread," and daily Communion became the rule in the Carmel of Lisieux. Mother Gonzague was also won over to the practice. Had Thérèse not said to her, "Mother, when I am in heaven, I'll get you to change your ideas"?

The "Little Queen" had even added mysteriously: "You will see, when I get to heaven, there will be a change in the Church's practice regarding Holy Communion." It was to her eldest sister, her godmother, Sister Marie du Sacré Coeur, that she said this, and many have not hesitated to attribute to the intercession of St. Thérèse the wonderful decrees of St. Pius X on Communion and the Communion of children.

This life-giving conception of the Blessed Eucharist is a central point in the doctrine of St. Thérèse. We may rightly ask why did she aspire to daily union with the Divine Victim? It was to correspond with the desire of God Himself. It was above all to please Jesus Christ. The personal advantage to herself was eclipsed by her ardent desire to correspond with the plans of Merciful Love. Needless to say, the soul's interests are best safeguarded thereby also; in seeming to lose herself she gains all.

Our Lord doesn't come down from heaven every day just to wait there in a gold ciborium: He has found a much better heaven for His resting place; a Christian soul, made in His own image, the living temple of the Blessed Trinity. —*St. Thérèse*

How can we conceive the divine plan which leads up to the mystery of the Cenacle? Thérèse outlined it in her sublime address to her adorable Divine Eagle: "O Eternal Word! Thou art the Divine Eagle Whom I love and Who drawest me upward to Thyself. Descending to this land of exile, Thou didst will to suffer and to die, in order to bear away each single soul and plunge it into the very heart of the Blessed Trinity — eternal Home of Love! Returning to Thy realm of light, Thou dost still remain hidden here in our vale of tears, under the appearance of the white Host, to nourish me with Thy own substance, poor little creature that would return to its nothingness if Thy divine gaze did not uphold my life from moment to moment." She has expressed the same thought in one of her poems:

Remember we were not left orphans here
When to Thy Father Thou didst go, and mine:
Thou mad'st Thyself a Prisoner on earth,

Veiling the radiance of Thy light divine.

And yet the veil, dear Lord, is luminous and clear

O living Bread of faith, Our Food celestial here.

Love's mystery! From Heaven

My daily bread is given

And, Jesus, it is Thou!

At her second Communion, two weeks after the first, Thérèse said: "I recalled and repeated again and again the words of St. Paul: 'It is not I who live — it is Christ Who lives in me.'" The logic of the divine plan urges the intensive use of this sovereign remedy: daily recourse to this means which *Christifies* us. In that light the daily bread of the *Our Father* assumes a new brilliancy and the shadow of objections fades away. Our unworthiness? Thérèse gives the key argument in her Little Way. Our misery and poverty are lodestones which draw down Merciful Love. "The Guest of our soul knows our misery; He comes to find an empty tent within us — that is all He asks."

As a penalty for some fault, a novice wished to deprive herself of Holy Communion. St. Thérèse wrote her this note: "Instead of closing up the corolla of your heart, you should open it out, that the Bread of Angels may come to nourish you and give you all you need." Is anyone afraid of apathy, lukewarmness, of going to Communion without feeling, in the dark, as it were? Thérèse quickly puts aside the objection. "Do not be troubled," she writes to her cousin, "if you do not feel any consolation; it is a trial we must bear with patience and love." Thérèse herself had passed through that crucible.

Again she writes: "What shall I say of my thanksgiving? There is no time when I feel less consolation! Again is that not quite natural, since I do not desire the visit of Our Lord for my own satisfaction, but solely for His pleasure." Let us underline that last word. It reveals the essential, "theocentric" attitude of Thérèse: always, and above all, it is the pleasure of the good God — the glory of God that she seeks. In preparing for Holy Communion, she does not rely on her own virtues; she begs the Blessed Virgin to prepare her for the great Visit. "All that does not prevent distractions and sleepiness from annoying me; and so, very frequently I make the resolution to continue my thanksgiving during the whole day, since I made it so badly in the morning."

Marie Guerin was not so easily convinced. Her uneasy conscience, tortured by scruples, kept her from approaching the Holy Table. A letter from Thérèse, May 30, 1889, as forceful as it was kind in expression, reveals Thérèse's whole mind on the subject. She wrote: "The devil must indeed be clever to deceive a soul like that . . . .But surely you know,

> **She often expressed a certain regret at her own exclusion from the priesthood, and in June 1897 when she knew her illness was fatal, she naively said to me: "The Good God is taking me to Heaven before the age when ordination usually is taking place; He must want to spare me the chagrin of witnessing the actual frustration of my ardent desire to be a priest....What marvels shall we not behold in Heaven! I truly believe that those who have so lovingly desired the priesthood and have not attained to it in this world will enjoy all its privileges in the next.**
> —Sister Geneviève of the Holy Face, *A Memoir of My Sister St. Thérèse*

darling, that this is the one goal of his desires. He realizes, treacherous creature that he is, that he cannot get a soul to sin, if that soul belongs wholly to Jesus, so he only tries to make it think it is in sin. He has already done much when he puts confusion into that soul; but his rage demands something more. He wants to deprive Jesus of a loved tabernacle. Since he cannot enter that sanctuary himself, he wants at least to have it remain empty, and without master!

"Alas! what will become of that poor heart? When the devil has succeeded in keeping a soul away from Holy Communion, he has gained all...and Jesus weeps! O my darling, do you realize that Jesus is there in the tabernacle expressly for you — for you alone. He burns with the desire to come into your heart... don't listen to the demon, laugh at him, and go without fear to receive the Jesus of peace and love...Dearest little Sister, receive Communion often, very often...there you have the sole remedy, if you want to be cured. Jesus has not put this attraction into your heart for nothing..."

That testimony, hurriedly traced out by a Carmelite Sister at the age of sixteen and a half, at a time when learned theologians were cautiously considering the frequency of Communions, was brought to the notice of St. Pius X, by Msgr. de Teil, Vice-Postulator of the Cause of St Thérèse. The Holy Father was deeply impressed. "That is most welcome," he cried, "most opportune! Oh, what a joy that gives me. We must advance her cause quickly." Is it not appropriate that we associate together the "Pope of the Eucharist" and St. Thérèse, who prayed so trustingly and fervently for his Decrees?

A slightly condensed version from Sicut Parvuli,
reprinted with permission.

The Pope visits Lisieux on June 2, 1980. In his Apostolic Letter, *Divini Amoris Scientia,* October 19, 1997, on the occasion of St. Thérèse becoming a Doctor of the Church, the Holy Father points out: "Her teaching not only conforms to Scripture and the Catholic Faith, but excells for the depth and wise synthesis it achieved. Her doctrine is at once a confession of the Church's faith, and experience of the Christian mystery and a way of holiness. Thérèse offers a mature synthesis of Christian spirituality: she combines theology and the spiritual life; she expresses herself with strength and authority, with a great ability to persuade and communicate, as is shown by the reception and dissemination of her message among the People of God."

Important Biographical Dates

1873   JANUARY 2: Marie-Françoise Thérèse Martin is born in Alençon.

JANUARY 4: She is baptized in the Church of Notre-Dame.

1877   AUGUST 28: Zelie Martin dies.

NOVEMBER 16: The Martins move to Lisieux (Les Buissonnets).

1881   OCTOBER 3: Thérèse become a day-boarder at the Benedictine school of Notre-Dame du Pre.

1882   OCTOBER 2: Pauline Martin enters the Carmel in Lisieux.

1883   MARCH 25: Thérèse falls gravely ill.

MAY 13: The Virgin smiles on her and she is cured.

1884   MAY 8: She receives her First Holy Communion, followed by Confirmation on June 14.

1885   MAY: The beginning of a period of scruples.

1886   FEBRUARY: She falls ill, is taken out of school and tutored.

OCTOBER 15: Marie Martin enters the Carmel at Lisieux.

DECEMBER 25: The "Conversion" of Thérèse on Christmas eve.

1887   AUGUST: Her prayers for conversion of the murderer Pranzini are heard.

OCTOBER 31: She has an audience with Msgr. Hugonin to seek permission to enter Carmel in Lisieux.

NOV. 4 to DEC. 2: The Martins (Louis, Celine and Thérèse) on pilgrimage.

1888   APRIL 9: She enters the Lisieux Carmel at the age of fifteen.

JUNE 23-27 Louis Martin runs away and is found in Le Havre.

1889   JANUARY 10: Thérèse is clothed in the Carmelite habit.

FEBRUARY 12: Louis Martin is admitted to Bon Sauveur hospital in Caen.

JULY: Special grace of awareness of Mary's presence.

1890   SEPTEMBER 8: Thérèse takes her vows.

SEPTEMBER 24: She receives the Veil in a public ceremony.

1891   OCTOBER: The retreat conducted by Father Prou launches her on the way of complete trust and abandon. She begins reading St. John of the Cross.

WINTER of 1891-1892: In a severe influenza epidemic, several nuns die.

1892   MAY 10: Louis Martin returns to Lisieux.

1893   FEBRUARY 20: Sister Agnes of Jesus (Pauline Martin) is elected prioress.

1894   JULY 29: Louis Martin dies.

SEPTEMBER 14: Céline Martin enters the Carmel, and is entrusted to Thérèse.

DECEMBER: On the instructions of her prioress, Thérèse begins writing her childhood memories.

1895   Manuscript A is completed this year.

JUNE 9: She makes the Act of Oblation to God's Merciful Love.

JUNE 11: In making the Stations of the Cross she experiences the "Wound of Love."

OCTOBER 17: Seminarian Maurice Belliere is entrusted to Thérèse's care.

1896   JANUARY 20: Thérèse brings Mother Agnes her memories (manuscript A).

MARCH 17: Sister Geneviève (Celine) receives the Veil.

MARCH 21: Mother Marie de Gonzague is elected Prioress, and entrusts her five novices to Thérèse.

APRIL 2-3: Holy Thursday night, she experiences her first hemorrhage.

APRIL 5: Easter Sunday or shortly after, she enters into the great trial of faith and hope which lasts to her death.

MAY 30: Father Roulland is entrusted to her as her second spiritual brother.

SEPTEMBER 8: She begins writing part B, addressed to Jesus. Manuscript B is dedicated to her sister, Sr. Marie of the Sacred Heart.

1897   APRIL: Towards the end of Lent Thérèse enters into her final, painful illness.

APRIL 6: Her sisters begin recording her last conversations.

JUNE 3: Mother Gonzague orders Thérèse to write manuscript C.

JULY 8: She enters the infirmary.

JULY 30: Thérèse receives the Last Rites.

AUGUST 19: She receives Communion for the last time.

SEPTEMBER 30: She dies around 7 p.m. after a prolonged agony.

OCTOBER 4: She is buried in Lisieux cemetery.

After her Death

1898   SEPTEMBER 30: Two thousand copies of her autobiography "Story of a Soul" are published.

1899-1902 The first pilgrims to Thérèse's grave and first miracles and cures reported.

1923   Her relics are moved to the Carmel in Lisieux.

APRIL 29: She is beatified by Pius XI.

1925   MAY 17: The canonization by Pope Pius XI takes place in St. Peter's before an audience of 60,000, with 500,000 in the square.

1927   DECEMBER 14: Pius XI names her co-patroness of the Missions along with St. Francis Xavier.

1929   SEPTEMBER 30: The first stone is laid for the Basilica in Lisieux.

1937   JULY 11: The Basilica is inaugurated.

1944   MAY 3: Pius XII proclaims Thérèse Second Patron Saint of France.

1947	Fiftieth anniversary of Thérèse's death.
	Her relics are taken to nearly all the dioceses in France.
1956	Facsimile edition is published of the original manuscripts of the "Story of a Soul."
1973	The centenary year of her birth is celebrated.
1980	JUNE 2: John Paul II goes on a pilgrimage to Lisieux.
1971-1988	The "Centenary Edition," the critical edition of Thérèse's "Complete Works," is published. Restoration of the original writing of "Story of a Soul" by Fr. François de Sainte-Marie.
1993	AUGUST 2: New "Centenary Edition" is presented to Pope John Paul II
1997	Centenary year of the death of St. Thérèse.
	OCTOBER 16: St. Thérèse of the Infant Jesus and the Holy Face is declared a Doctor of the Catholic Church.

The Basilica of St. Thérèse dominates the skyline of the city of Lisieux. In the foreground, just a short distance from the Basilica, is the Carmel where St. Thérèse spent the last nine years of her life.

Recommended Available Sources

BOOKS

I C S Publications, 2131 Lincoln Road, NE, Washington, DC 21077-0572

Story of Soul: The Autobiography of St. Thérèse of Lisieux. Translated by John Clarke, OCD. Paperback, 300 pages. The most accurate translation from the French which includes index and eight pages of photos. ($11.95)

St. Thérèse of Lisieux: Her Last Conversations. Translated by John Clarke, OCD. Paperback, 352 pages. Includes general and Biblical index and twelve photos. ($11.95)

The Letters of St. Thérèse and Those Who Knew Her. Vol. I. General Correspondence I. Translated from the critical edition by John Clarke, OCD. Paperback, 700 pages. ($16.95)

The Letters of St. Thérèse of Lisieux and Those Who Knew Her. Vol. II General Correspondence II. Translated from the critical edition by John Clarke, OCD. Paperback, 788 pages. Includes an index for Vol. I and Vol. II. ($16.95)

The Poetry of St. Thérèse of Lisieux. Translated by Donald Kinney, OCD. Paperback, 352 pages. This is the first English translation of the complete poems of Thérèse from the French critical edition. Both the French and excellent English texts are included. ($12.95)

The Prayers of St. Thérèse of Lisieux. Translated by Aletheia Kane, OCD. Paperback, 108 pages, 1997. Collected for the first time in English, all twenty-one prayers by Thérèse. ($9.95)

St. Thérèse of Lisieux: Her Life, Times, and Teaching. Compiled by the Discalced Carmelite Friars. Hard cover, 300 pages, 1997. This elegant volume provides a clear introduction to the message and meaning of St. Thérèse for today. ($44.95)

Carmelite Studies: Experiencing St. Thérèse Today. Edited by John Sullivan, OCD. Paperback, 220 pages, 1990. Contains eleven essays on the Saint's life, spirituality, and writings. ($9.95)

Tan Books and Publishers, Inc., Rockford, Illinois 61105

The Story of a Family. The Home of St. Thérèse of Lisieux. By Stephane-Joseph Piat, OFM. Paperback, 459 pages. Shows how holy parents and a wonderful family life produced a saint ($18.50).

St. Thérèse, The Little Flower - The Making of a Saint. By John Beevers. Paperback, 157 pages. By stressing the Saint's upbringing, this biography explains how Thérèse became a great saint. ($6.00)

Thoughts of St. Thérèse. Translated from the French *Pensées* by an Irish Carmelite. Paperback, 180 pages. Composed of 328 brief quotations under twenty different topics from the Saint's own words. ($6.00)

My Sister Saint Thérèse. By Sister Geneviève of the Holy Face (Céline Martin). Paperback, 250 pages. This is the authorized translation of *Counsels and Reminiscences,* a treasury of memories, teachings, anecdotes, and conversations written down by the Saint's sister before and during Thérèse's last days. ($6.00)

The Story of a Soul: The Autobiography of Saint Thérèse of Lisieux. Edited by Mother Agnes of Jesus (Thérèse's sister) and translated by Michael Day, Cong. Orat. Paperback, 220 pages, illustrated, 1997. This was first published in English in 1951. ($8.00)

Leaflet Missal Company, 976 South Seton Drive, South Holland, IL 60473

Léonie Martin: A Difficult Life. Written by Marie Baudouin-Croix and translated by Mary Frances Mooney. Paperback, 128 pages, illustrated, 1993. The emotionally troubled Martin sister who became a Visitation nun followed faithfully the Little Way and died a holy death ($9.95)

Thérèse and Lisieux. Text by Pierre Descouvemont, photographs by Helmuth Nils Loose. Translated from the French by Salvatore Sciurba, OCD, and Louise Pambrun. Hard cover, 336 pages, 600 photo-documents. A unique pictorial history of St. Thérèse from birth to canonization and beyond, illustrated in color with magnificent reproductions of photos, documents, and art work. ($49.95)

The Photo Album of St. Thérèse of Lisieuix. Commentary by François de Sainte-Marie, OCD, and translation by Peter-Thomas Rohrbach, OCD. Hard cover, 224 pages, illustrated. A superb volume of all 47 photographs taken of St. Thérèse. ($24.95)

Ignatius Press, P.O. Box 1339, Fort Collins, Colorado 80522

Céline: Sister Geneviève of the Holy Face, Sister and Witness to St. Thérèse of the Child Jesus. By Stephane-Joseph Piat, OFM, and translated by the Carmelite Sisters of the Eucharist of Colchester, Connecticut. Paperback, 201 pages, illustrated. This biography of the Saint's closest sister and friend reveals her great influence on Thérèse. ($12.95)

Two Sisters in the Spirit: Thérèse of Lisieux and Elizabeth of the Trinity. By Hans Urs Von Balthasar and translated by Donald Nichol. Paperback, 499 pages. Fine biography and explanation of St. Thérèse's spirituality by a well known theologian and scholar. ($19.95)

St. Thérèse of Lisieux By Those Who Knew Her. Edited and translated by Christopher O'Mahony. Paperback, 287 pages. Excellent testimonies from fifteen people who knew the Saint and gave witness at the Process of Beatification. ($14.95)

Harper & Row, Publishers, Inc., 10 East 53rd Street, New York, NY 10022

The Story of a Life: St. Thérèse of Lisieux. By Msgr. Guy Gaucher, OCD and translated by Sister Anne Marie Brennan, OCD. Hard cover, 228 pages, illustrated. Excellent biography covering every detail of St. Thérèse's life and spirituality written by the leading Thérèsian scholar and presently Auxiliary Bishop of Lisieux.

Liguori Publications, One Liguori Drive, Liguori, MO 63057-9999

Thérèse of Lisieux: A Life of Love. By Jean Chalon and translated by Anne Collier Rehill. Paperback, 276 pages, illustrated, 1997. Very readable biography supported by impeccable scholarship. ($16.00)

Alba House, Society of St. Paul, 2187 Victory Blvd., Staten Island, New York 10314

Complete Spiritual Doctrine of St. Thérèse of Lisieux. By Rev. Francois Jamart, OCD, translated by Rev. Walter Van de Putte, CSSP. Paperback, 320 pages, 1961. ($16.95)

Pauline Books and Media, Daughters of St. Paul, 50 St. Paul's Avenue, Boston, MA 02130-3491

St. Thérèse of Lisieux From Lisieux to the Four Corners of the World. Text by Msgr. Guy Gaucher, OCD. Paperback, forty-eight pages, illustrated. A magnificent overview of her life, spirituality, and her world influence with testimonials from various leading world figures. (USA $9.50 - Canada $14.25)

St. Theresa the Little Flower. By Sr. Gesualda of the Holy Spirit. Paperback, 205 pages. A warm story of the young Saint who continues to draw people to God through her "Little Way" of love and confidence. (USA $9.95 - Canada $14.95)

Call Me Little Theresa, St. Theresa of Lisieux. By Susan Helen Wallace, FSP. with beautiful illustrations by Nino Musio on the life of St. Thérèse for young people.

OTHER

St. Therese, Martyr of Love, By Rev. Herbert Schmidt. Paperback, 112 pages, with extensive Chapter Notes, and good Bibliography. The author is an apostle of St. Thérèse who has other promotion material as well. His address is: 47 Pine Street, West Springfield, MA 01089

The Message of St. Teresa of Lisieux, By Msgr. Vernon Johnson. This compact little booklet of 64 pages covers the Little Way applying the relationship of small children to their parents to the Little Way. Two of the chapters of this book are taken from this booklet. Catholic Truth Society, 38/40 Eccleston Square, London S.W.1 England. (£1.95)

PERIODICALS

Apostolate of The Little Flower. A national Catholic bimonthly, with articles and lists of favors received through St. Thérèse, published by the Discalced Carmelite Fathers, P.O. Box 5280, San Antonio, Texas 78201-0280. (No subscription fee)

Sicut Parvuli. Published by the Association of St. Thérèse, 68 Northdown Park Road, Cliftonville, Margate, Kent CT9 3PT, England. A British magazine issued quarterly covering all aspects of St. Thérèse's life, spirituality, and message.

Leaves. A bi-monthly magazine published by the Marianhill Fathers, listing favors received through St. Thérèse and featuring articles about her. P.O. Box 87, Dearborn, MI 48121-0087. (No subscription fee)

AUDIO TAPES AND VIDEO CASSETTES

St. Joseph Communications, Inc, P.O. Box 720, West Covina, CA 91793

The Saint for Me and Mass Homily by Bishop Patrick Ahern. Reflections on Thérèse, the friendliest of saints, God's mercy, her "Little Way", and her approach to Scripture. ($7.50)

Upon visiting the Bishop to ask permission to enter the austere Carmelite order at fifteen, St. Thérèse arranged her hair to look older. She told the Bishop that she wanted to be a religious since the dawn of her reason.

Reflected in the mirror is the room in which Our Lady appeared and cured St. Thérèse. The statue of Our Lady of the Smile is on the left.

The Little Way to Spiritual Heights by Sr. Carmelina Leland, OCD. An in-depth analysis of Thérèse's doctrine of spiritual childhood as seen in her life and teaching.

St. Thérèse's Message for Today by Fr. Thomas Koller, OCD. Explains why St. Thérèse is another Joan of Arc and how God's mercy sums up Thérèse's life, message, and mission.

(All the above 3 audio tapes for $19.95)

Pauline Books and Media, Daughters of St. Paul, 50 St. Paul's Avenue, Boston, MA 02130-3491

Story of a Soul: The Autobiography of St. Thérèse of Lisieux. A reading of the entire book on nine video cassettes. (USA $49.95 - Canada $74.95)

St. Thérèse, The Little Flower: Spiritual Childhood and Sanctity. By Bishop Patrick V. Ahern who discusses the spiritual journey of the Saint and her great confidence in God's merciful love. On one 45 minute audio cassette. (USA $7.95 - Canada $11.95)

St. Thérèse of Lisieux: From Her Heart to Your Heart. By Sr. Debra-Therese Carroll, CT, who explores Thérèse's spirituality and confidence in God's love and mercy in a unique first-person manner. One 20 minute video cassette. (USA $19.95 - Canada $29.95)

Further Information from the Publishers of
St. Thérèse, Doctor of the Church

The Franciscan Friars of the Immaculate, publishers of *St. Thérèse, Doctor of the Little Way, A Handbook on Guadalupe* and other books on the Eucharist and Our Lady, walk in the footsteps of St. Maximilian Kolbe, the hero of Auschwitz. They concentrate their efforts in the mass media to further the reign of the Sacred Heart of Jesus through total consecration to Mary Immaculate.

The Academy of the Immaculate, a non-profit Roman Catholic organization for the promotion of the theological studies of the Immaculate Virgin, works in collaboration with the Franciscan Friars of the Immaculate. Some of the recent publications of the Friars and the Academy are:

All Generations Shall Call Me Blessed: *A Biblical Mariology* by Fr. Stefano Manelli, F.I. 393 pp. ($19.95)

Totus Tuus: *Pope John Paul II's Program of Marian Consecration and Entrustment* by Msgr. Arthur Calkins 334 pp. ($14.95)

For the Life of the World: *St. Maximilian Kolbe and the Eucharist* by Fr. Jerzy Domanski, O.F.M. Conv. 160 pp. ($8.95)

Jesus, Our Eucharistic Love: *Eucharistic Life As Exemplified by the Saints* by Fr. Stephano Manelli, F.I. 118 pp. ($5.00)

A Handbook on Guadalupe: *A Comprehensive Coverage of Guadalupe* Edited by a Friar of the Immaculate 240 pp. ($12.50)

St. Thérèse, Doctor of the Little Way: *A compilation of the past and latest on the New Doctor of the Church* Edited by a Friar of the Immaculate, 180 pp. ($9.50)

Virgo Facta Ecclesia — St. Francis of Assisi and His Charism: *A brief biography on the Saint with reflections on his charism for our times* by the Franciscans of the Immaculate.

When ordering these books please include along with your payment, postage and handling as follows:
In the USA and Canada: $2.00 for the first book, .75c for each additional book.
Other countries: $5.00 for first book, $1.00 for each additional book.

For single copies & special rates for parishes and religious organizations write:
Academy of the Immaculate, POB 667, Valatie, NY 12184
Or phone/FAX (518) 758-1584, E-mail - Mimike@pipeline.com

For quotations on attractive bulk rates, shipped directly from the printery contact: Friars of the Immaculate, (508) 984-1856, FAX (508) 996-8296, E-mail - ffi@ici.net